THE FUND

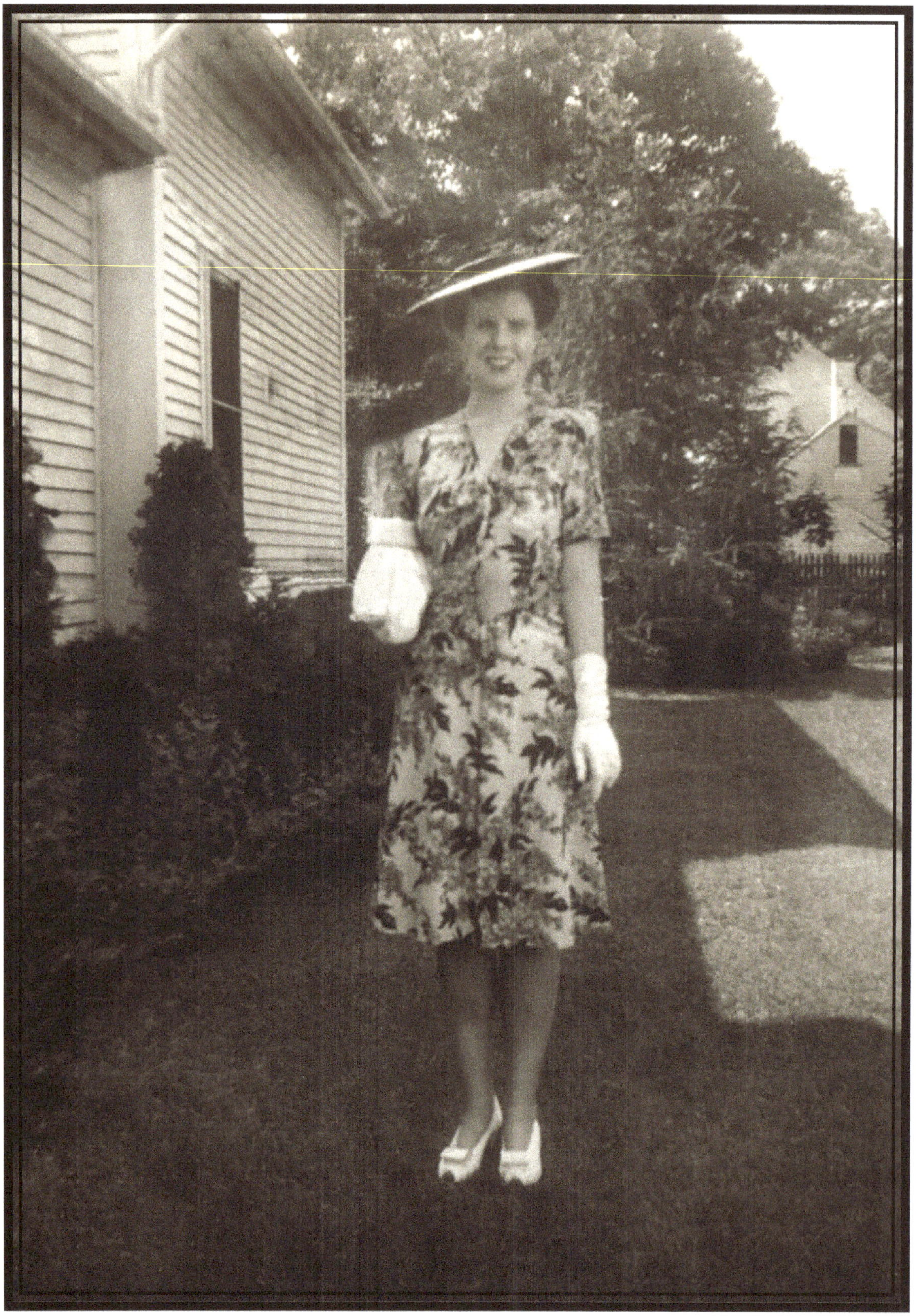

THE FUND

A MEMOIR OF MOM

CHARLENE KANE DIAZ

Disclaimer

This work depicts actual events in my life as truthfully as recollection permits and/or can be verified by research. No names have been changed, no characters invented, no events fabricated. I have tried to recreate events, locales and conversations from my memories of them.

PALMETTO
PUBLISHING
Charleston, SC
www.PalmettoPublishing.com

Copyright © 2024 by Charlene Kane Diaz

All rights reserved

No portion of this book may be reproduced, stored in a retrieval system, or transmitted in any form by any means–electronic, mechanical, photocopy, recording, or other–except for brief quotations in printed reviews, without prior permission of the author.

Hardcover ISBN: 9798822937765
Paperback ISBN: 9798822937772

For Mom

THE FUND

This memoir of our mother was inspired by a TV show entitled, *I Remember Mama.*

"The series told the ongoing story of a loving Norwegian family living in San Francisco in the 1910s through the eyes of the elder daughter, Katrin Hansen. Katrin would be seen looking through the pages of the family album at the start of each episode with the opening narration:

'This old album makes me remember so many things in the past. San Francisco and the house on Steiner Street where I was born. It brings back memories of my cousins, aunts and uncles; all the boys and girls I grew up with. And I remember my family as we were then. My big brother Nels, my little sister Dagmar, and of course, Papa. **But most of all, when I look back to those days so long ago, most of all, I remember ... Mama.**'"

**Mom always said, "Write about what you know."
Although she was indescribable, I'll do my best.**

Mom

> "The best protection any woman can have…is courage."
> Elizabeth Cady Stanton

THE FUND

My mother always told me that a woman needs financial independence - cash she could put her hands on immediately in case of an emergency. And, if she were married, that special reserve should be secret, hidden from everyone – especially her husband (not a notion to which I have subscribed). I think my mother may have had misgivings about men, understandably so because of her extraordinary dealings with them throughout her life. More about that later. As the sole caretaker of two daughters, she was a single parent (sort of) during an era when all families looked like they came from the land of *Leave It to Beaver*. At any rate, she was determined to have a contingency plan no matter what. She started by saving at least $1.00 from her paycheck every week (a decent amount since she began working just after The Great Depression). And so, **The Fund** began.

I didn't hear about The Fund until my mother and I took a trip to Cape Cod in the late eighties. We had a great time, and Mom suggested that we save money each week so that we could take similar trips in the future. We each put in $10.00 every Friday. She said we would call it The Fund. She told me that was the way she "funded" all the trips we took throughout our lives, and we took LOTS of them. This was her philosophy:

> Never ask of money spent
> Where the spender thinks it went.
> Nobody was ever meant
> To remember or invent
> What he did with every cent.
>
> Robert Frost

However, The Fund did much more than satisfy our wanderlust. It sustained us through thick and thin and made it possible to triumph over adversity.

CONTENTS

Chapter 01. *MEXICO* *1*

Chapter 02. *ROME* *25*

Chapter 03. *3 B'S AND A CON MAN* *47*

Chapter 04. *RAHAR'S INN* *79*

Chapter 05. *Sylvie* *95*

Chapter 06. *ALBERT* *113*

Chapter 07. *Bats in the Belfry: The Clinic* *137*

Chapter 08. *HOW PEOPLE GRIEVE* *161*

Chapter 09. *The Most Beautiful Woman I Ever Saw* *181*

Chapter 10. *"Most of All, We Remember Mom"* *209*

Acknowledgements *217*

APPENDICES *219*

NOTES *231*

Photo Credits *239*

Chapter One

"MEXICO"

The first big trip we took was to Mexico City in the summer of 1961. We went with a man I called my Godfather. We always referred to him as The Doctor and as Babbo at home. Our lives were intertwined for decades. My mother worked for him for thirty years as a nurse/surgical technician in the operating room. He wouldn't let anyone else assist him. The others couldn't put up with him shouting orders and throwing tools when things were not done perfectly. Later, she supervised the Furcolo Clinic which he created after giving up surgery. He sustained a leg injury and could no longer perform operations which required several hours of standing in one spot. So, he started a medical clinic – a true forerunner to the ubiquitous urgent care facilities we see today.

The Doctor was a very successful physician listed in all the *Who's Who* books. They said he had eyes on his fingertips – that he could remove an appendix with a tiny incision only ¼ inch long. My mother told us he invented the procedure.

He was also the sole doctor for the entire Italian community in the city including "***La Familia***" which often resulted in fringe benefits for all of us. Whenever we dined in the South End, dinner was on the house!

Dr. Charles L. Furcolo

Mom at Mercy Hospital

There was an incident that sealed that relationship according to Mom. Whether or not it really happened, I don't know. The Irish are great storytellers, and Mom was one of the best. She appreciated the art of embellishment – or what the Irish often refer to as "blarney." According to the story, there was a shooting in the South End. It happened to be in front of The Doctor's first office on Union and Main. Since help was needed immediately to care for the victim, someone ran upstairs and got The Doctor. As the story goes, he rushed downstairs and just happened to place his medical bag on top of the revolver that was next to the victim. Later, when the ambulance arrived, The Doctor picked up his medical bag **along with the revolver** and the weapon disappeared. Apparently, that was helpful to the parties involved. The Doctor was a "made man" after that (which came in handy a few years later).

The Doctor drove a big white Cadillac Coupe Deville with long tail-fin wings. That's the car we drove, **yes drove**, all the way from Massachusetts to Mexico City! (No wonder the people in Mexico thought he was the President.) We made several stops along the way. I remember the segregated South and getting yelled at because we sat at the "wrong counter" in a luncheonette (reserved for "colored people"). As a young ten-year old brought up in the North in "mixed" schools, I became very pensive (for lack of a better word) as we walked through the streets of the small town with segregated bathrooms and drinking fountains. Little did I know how this would shape my character in years to come.

Another striking memory was hearing men in business suits speaking with a heavy accent. The juxtaposition of professionalism with a Southern drawl was confusing. Not that we spoke the Queen's English up North, but we thought that everyone "educated" spoke the way we did. "Studies have shown that whether you are from the North or South, a Southern twang pegs the speaker as comparatively dimwitted, but also likely to be a nicer person than folks who speak like a Yankee." (*Scientific American*) Interesting. To this day, I'm still perplexed when I hear politicians from the South but charmed when I hear the Southern belles (voted the sexiest accent in the U.S. on social media).

The most exciting stop was New Orleans. We ate at a restaurant in the French Quarter called The Court of the Two Sisters (**special for us because my sister, Nora, and I were also two sisters**). Dining in a courtyard blanketed with lavender wisteria and vibrant red and green parrots in elaborate wrought iron cages, we were enchanted. The history is that two sisters, Bertha Angaud and Emma Connors, who belonged to a well-known Creole family, set up a shop in 1886 and made it possible for the city's finest women to be well-appointed with the latest fashion trends. The sisters would occasionally serve tea to their very special customers in the beautiful courtyard. Today, The Court of the Two Sisters is known for New Orleans jazz, delicious Creole cuisine, and its picturesque patio. Thankfully, it survived Hurricane Katrina.

Nora

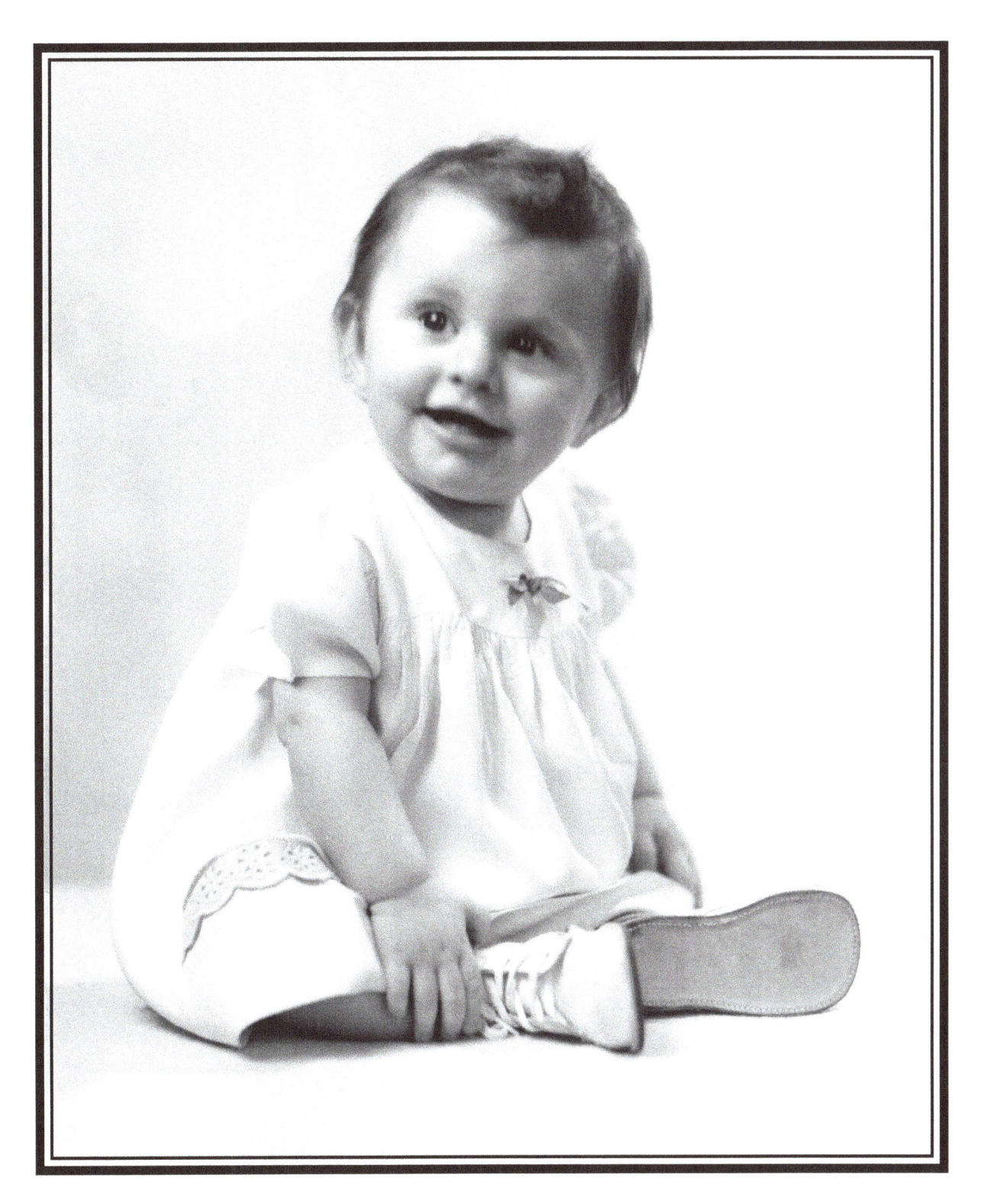

Charlene

The two sisters

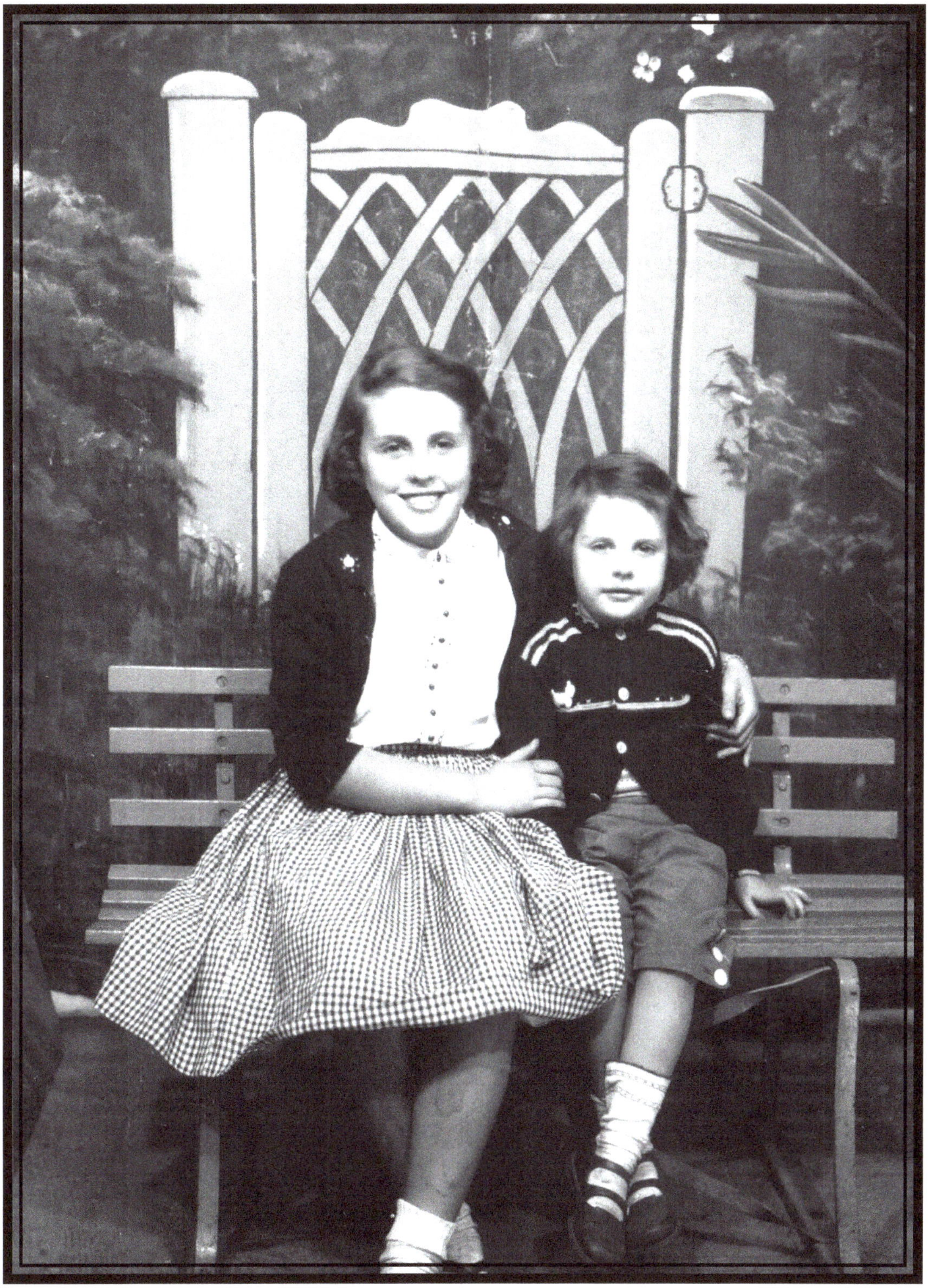

The Court of the Two Sisters Restaurant in New Orleans

The French Quarter in New Orleans

Next stop – The Alamo – not as moving! Remember the Alamo? I wanted to forget it! I was probably too young to be interested in this fortress which became a symbol of independence of Texas from Mexico. I didn't realize until today that it's located in San Antonio. I think we should have relocated to the city's vibrant and colorful River Walk jam-packed with lively restaurants, outdoor cafes peppered with multi-colored umbrellas, ornate walking bridges, and unique shops.

After that, we crossed the Rio Grande River and the Mexican border. Later in life, every time we talked too much and revealed something that should have remained private, my mother would say, "Remember that river…**Boca Grande** (big mouth)." It was her code that we should stop talking immediately! She never wanted us to answer ANY questions that people might ask. Her life was private, and most might not have understood the choices she made. Just say, "I don't know!"

Our first stop before the CLIMB into the mountains was Monterrey. My mother disappeared for a while searching for a wonderful restaurant for dinner. She often explored on her own and then took us to all the exciting places. After our visit, she wrote a poem about our stay there. My sister needed to write one for an assignment in school, so she submitted Mom's and won all kinds of awards!

Monterrey, Mexico

Surrounded by the purpliest mountains
I have ever seen,
With their snowcapped noses poked up
Between
The clouds and mists of crystal air,
Early one morning, I roamed your quaint
And picturesque streets.
Colors I had visioned only in dreams,
Greeted me everywhere.
Even the sidewalks gleamed, in shades
Of red and gold and green.
Soon gay serapes and market day chatter
Invaded my fairyland.
The strains of the strings resumed and
I knew the town had awaken.
And I was called to continue on my way.

My mother wrote poetry a lot and did extensive research to prepare for this trip and all other trips. She was also an avid reader. Later in life when we went to flea markets and yard sales, she would painstakingly peruse the shelves. She rarely found new books to read because she had read them all. She must have read about Mexico City in one of them because that often prompted her desire to visit all the exciting places that became the destinations of later trips – all possible because of The Fund.

We continued our journey up and down mountains with narrow, one-lane roads and very steep cliffs. It was a LONG trip. The Doctor could get by in Italian wherever we would stop. People in the small towns were fascinated with the big white Cadillac and were eager to help us navigate whenever we were lost. It seemed like days to get from Monterrey to Mexico City. It was more than 500 miles and ten hours of driving.

We stayed overnight at the Tuna Motel. It had a small swimming pool, but the only thing in it was a gigantic insect about four inches long – must have been the beetle species known as a Giant Water Bug. Very scary! Needless to say, we didn't go swimming.

We finally arrived in Mexico City. It was bustling and exciting. There were huge, ten-story mosaic tile murals on the entire façade of buildings in the middle of the city. Equally impressive were the floating gardens at Xochimilco – the "Venice of Mexico." The floating gardens are a UNESCO (United Nations Educational, Scientific and Cultural Organization) World Heritage Site where you can ride around the canals on colorful gondola-like *trajineras,* sample the local cuisine, and be serenaded by *mariachis*. The "floating gardens" were actually agricultural "fields" embedded in wetlands by the Aztecs. Fascinating!

Back in the city, we endured fifteen minutes of a bull fight because my mother was horrified by the torture of the bulls. We made a grand exit at the most exciting moment climbing over all the spectators. They weren't very happy. We were 100% with her and The Doctor had to follow. **She was leaving and that was that!**

There was a joke in Mexico – steak is always better on Monday (after the bullfights on Sunday). So, we went to an upscale restaurant and ate Chateaubriand prepared tableside.

We couldn't face the trip back over the mountains, so we hired our guide, George, to drive the Cadillac to the border. We took the train – one with sleeper cars and all-night parties just like in the movie *Some Like It Hot* with Marilyn Monroe, Jack Lemmon, and Tony Curtis. I sat up all night on the edge of my top bunk and joined the fun as fellow travelers laughed in amusement and passed around bottles of tequila (I didn't partake, I don't think). In the dining car, we tried to order some of that sweet, delicious pineapple available all over Mexico, but they brought us "pie apple" instead (apple pie). It wasn't quite the same. Some things were lost in translation.

Thankfully, our faithful guide arrived with the Cadillac, and we began the drive home with a stop in St. Louis, Missouri, to visit my mother's brother, Uncle Frank. He moved there straight out of the military because our VERY Catholic grandfather didn't approve of Uncle Frank's Protestant wife. It just wasn't done in those days. He became the editor of a newspaper, raised a family, and lived there for the rest of his life. Later, when my grandmother died, she left her house to my mother who had taken care of her for decades. That wasn't the only reason she left it to Mom. She knew my mother was basically on her own with two young girls. "Nanny" was probably the originator of my mother's special reserve and contingency plan. There was a difference of opinion between Mom and her brother about the house and who should get it. Much to their regret, they didn't speak again for forty years until just before Uncle Frank died! It was a phone call full of remorse because so much time had passed and of gratitude because a brother and a sister made amends. I don't remember who initiated the call. Too little, too late. He died before they could see each other again. She attended his funeral a few weeks later. Thankfully, Uncle Frank's daughter, our cousin Laura, developed a strong bond with Mom. They kept in close contact with each other for years. I think it eased the loss of her brother.

Be careful about those family spats. They can last a lifetime.

The Alamo

The San Antonio River Walk

Dinner in Monterrey, Mexico

A carriage ride in Monterrey

The Central Library at the University of Mexico in Mexico City

The Floating Gardens at Xochimilco – The Venice of Mexico

Our cousin, Laura, and Mom

Uncle Frank and Mom

Chapter Two

"ROME"

Only a few **months** later, in December of 1961, my 5th grade teacher came up to me in amazement and exclaimed, "YOU'RE GOING TO EUROPE! YOUR MOTHER IS COMING TO GET YOU!" I wasn't sure what was happening, but before I knew it, we were leaving school and heading to the Health Department to get a smallpox vaccination. Being a nurse, my mother was so smart to have us get the vaccine on our inner thighs instead of our outer arms where everyone else got them. She knew the scratching of the needle for the vaccination would leave a very noticeable lifelong scar. It didn't show on our inner thighs, and for the rest of our lives we had beautiful, unadorned arms to show off in sleeveless, summer tops and formal evening gowns.

I think it was the **same day** that our travel agent drove us to Bradley Field to leave for Orly Airport in Paris, France! My mother must have packed our clothes and everything else we needed to cross "the pond" to the Continent. Did we have passports? I remember there was one with both my picture and hers on it. Years later, we were able to get a passport in one day by going to Boston. Maybe there was some sort of "fast track" option in our local federal building.

Apparently, The Doctor had gone ahead to work out some sort of deal to introduce Bingo to Europe. Mom said the actor, Van Johnson, was in the picture somehow, and The Doctor met him to discuss the logistics of the business venture.

Nora

Charlene

Le Grand Hôtel de Paris and Le Café de la Paix

Did it result from his possible rapport with Organized Crime or the fact that his son was the Governor of Massachusetts at the time? All we knew was that my mother got an overseas phone call from The Doctor (exceptionally rare at the time) asking if she could be there before the week was out. Her real estate broker's license (yes, she did that too) was invaluable somehow, so tickets and more were provided for the trip – all expenses paid (supplemented by The Fund, I'm sure). Of course, my mother never went anywhere without her two girls, so we were on our way as well. Maybe we provided moral support, but I'm sure she wanted to expand our horizons more than anything else.

It was like a whirlwind when we arrived. Telephone calls were impossible. You had to get to an English-speaking operator, give them the number you wanted to call, and then put in the right amount of French money at a precise time. The taxi was worse. My sister and I were embarrassed to try out our school French to give him the address. My mother was so upset with us. Someone finally blurted out "*treize*" (thirteen), and we were on our way to **Le Grand Hôtel de Paris.**

It was a magnificent place with the deepest bathtubs we had ever seen along with heated towel racks and pull cords for assistance. Total luxury! Every morning we'd order hot chocolate and a **Croque Monsieur** – "the gentlemen's sandwich" – from the famous bistro around the corner, **Café de la Paix.** "The **Croque Monsieur** is the king of the grilled ham and cheese made with Béchamel sauce, baked ham, three cheeses (Gruyere, Swiss, and Parmesan), Dijon mustard and grilled to perfection until all the cheese oozes out." Fantastic!

We saw **La Tour Eiffel**, **Les Champs-Élysées**, **Notre-Dame**, and **Les Bouquinistes de la Seine** (the traditional book stalls along the Seine River reminiscent of the film, *Charade,* with Cary Grant and Audrey Hepburn). Believe it or not, we also had a PRIVATE viewing of the Mona Lisa in the Louvre! It was December in the sixties. There were no tourists, no lines, no ropes – just us. Today, the portrait hangs behind bullet-proof glass to protect it from the thousands of daily spectators. Of course, my mother told us all about **the smile**. We stood there for a while and looked at it. It seemed like the right thing to do.

My mother read EVERYTHING about Paris on the plane and proved to be a "***guide exceptionnelle.***" We were intrigued by **Les Halles** – the open-air food markets. Curious about the raw, uncovered small carcasses of meat hanging from one stall, we tried to ask what they were. Our basic French didn't get us very far. Finally, the vendor said, "Meow, Meow, Meow." We were somewhat speechless; we don't think he was kidding.

Les Bouquinistes de Paris – The Booksellers

Paris

The true "*experience enchanteresse*" is an encounter at a Parisian *parfumerie.* My mother kept a business card from one of the most well-known in the city called ***VINCENT sur 20 Rue Royale***. That's where she discovered Nina Ricci's most famous perfume, ***L'Air du Temps*** (Air of Time). Housed in a delicate, crystal bottle designed by Marc Lalique in the shape of twin doves, it became the fragrance of choice for the rest of her life. It suited her. Described by its creator, master perfumer Francis Fabron, it was the "essence of passion and elegance" – just like Mom. ***L'Air du Temps*** is still available over sixty years later but is now considered a "vintage" fragrance - difficult to find and very expensive ($150 for a small container of talc!). Whenever we get a whiff of ***L'Air du Temps***, it reminds us of her. It's just like the phenomenon described by Marcel Proust in *Remembrance of Things Past*. The senses have an uncanny ability to take us through time and space at warp speed to a special moment in the past.

Before we knew it, we were off to Rome by train! The dining cars were fantastic. They had tables with linen cloths and tuxedoed waiters who placed a "***piccolo***" of wine in front of each person – even the children. "When in Rome…."

We got a chuckle out of an incident in the passenger cars. We had just discovered hairspray in small aerosol containers for the first time at the *parfumerie* in Paris. Bouffant hairstyles were popular, and my sister, being a teenager, just loved this new innovation that kept everything in place. She swirled it round and round on the train until the other passengers kept mumbling "***insetto***" and "***bestiolina***" among themselves. They thought there was an infestation and she was dousing her hairdo with bug spray! Once we figured out what they were saying, we couldn't stop laughing.

When we finally arrived in Rome, it was pure elegance all the way. We stayed in the Grand Hotel right near Michelangelo's statue of Moses with Horns – so we thought. My mother explained that the "horns" really depicted rays of light, but to this day we continue to call it Moses with the Horns.

My mother was infatuated with Rome and all things Italian. Even though she was 100% Irish, she was never drawn to Ireland. She preferred the Mediterranean people – their warmth and their culture, not to mention the food. She said I ate homemade Tagliatelle with Bolognese Sauce every day for three weeks!

Mom became the local historian. We learned all about the mythical twins, Romulus and Remus, who were raised by a she-wolf and later founded the city. We traversed the Seven Hills of Rome on which the city was built, drove along the Apian Way, and visited the Sistine Chapel and the Vatican (of course). We scrambled out of the Catacombs faster than we left the bullfight in Mexico City. **My mother didn't like being underground AT ALL!** To recover, we headed to the famous *Via Veneto* where we sipped *aperitivos* and experienced *la dolce vita,* "the sweet life."

We've always preferred dining and shopping to history. (One time during a professional development trip to Boston, the teachers were given some free time to walk the Freedom Trail. I escaped into a taxi and took my own freedom trail to Legal Seafoods. My mother taught me well.) So, restaurants and bargains were on the top of our list in Rome. The Colosseum took a back seat to the surrounding street vendors selling beautiful cameos set in pure gold. The Fund came in handy there! My mother collected cameos throughout her life and had a beautiful assortment of them. Equally fascinating were all the cats who lived around the Colosseum. There were hundreds of them! In fact, they have been "deemed an official part of Rome's bio-heritage since 2001 and have been known to follow around Barak Obama, Russell Crowe, and Prince Harry!" They are known as *I Gatti di Roma*. If you don't believe me, watch the infamous cat announce the epic battle at the Colosseum between Bruce Lee and Chuck Norris in *The Way of the Dragon!*

At the other end of the spectrum was *Via Condotti* – the Rodeo Drive of Rome. It begins at the base of the Spanish Steps in *Piazza Espagna.* The Spanish Steps are a popular gathering place for tourists who can meet, linger, and take in beautiful views of the eternal city. We went there to visit one of Rome's most exclusive streets for, you guessed it, SHOPPING. My mother indulged and bought an elegant dress designed by the Fontana sisters – Zoe, Micol, and Giovanna - who introduced Italian fashion to the world. Even Anita Ekberg wore one of their creations in the film, *La Dolce Vita*. Mom wore the dress for years to all special events. I can picture it to this day. My mother always had a sense of style. She wore fashionable hats to everyday events, formal elbow-length gloves, and fur coats and stoles to more formal occasions. She had several types – mink, Persian lamb, even a fox stole with the head and four feet! Very strange.

Harry's Bar on the Via Veneto in Rome

I Gatti di Roma at the Colosseum

We dined at several memorable restaurants. **Da Meo Patacca** stood out from the rest. The stairs of the ivy-covered tavern led us down to a spacious, rustic wine cellar with vaulted ceilings, stone arches, and wood-burning grills with open flames. My mother asked for the menu to add to her collection from around the world which lined the walls in our "playroom" at home (a one thousand square-foot finished basement lined with knotty pine, wall-to-wall bookshelves, and a large bar). The menu was unique – deep red and gold and **three feet long** with colorful, hand-painted images of food and messages to the diner. The waiter held it close to his chest, reluctant to give it away, but we convinced him. We often received VIP treatment because The Doctor generously rewarded those who took good care of us. It wasn't just the impeccable service. He gave from his heart to those who were not always appreciated. Whatever the case, we came home with that menu.

Da Meo Patacca was located in "*Trastevere*" across the Tiber River just past the Vatican in Rome. It was a lively, Bohemian neighborhood something like an Italian Greenwich Village with inviting piazzas just teeming with charming, outdoor cafes and quaint restaurants. It was our type of place. Another establishment in the same area was Corsetti, designed like a ship and run by the same family since 1921. We ate grilled *gamberi grande* – the largest shrimp we had ever seen. Delicious!

We wrapped up our stay by taking a daytrip to Naples where The Doctor was able to meet his cousin. The Doctor had not been back to Italy in about sixty years since **his mother boarded a ship for Ellis Island ON HER OWN with her six small children**! They eventually settled in New Haven where The Doctor went to Yale University and the Yale School of Medicine. He always said that he did his last two years of high school and college at the same time, getting up at 4 a.m. every morning to study. One of his cousins, a woman, also became a physician. My mother repeatedly reminded us of that fact so we would believe that women could accomplish anything. Significantly, carved into the stone wall above the door of the bakery in Italy owned by The Doctor's family was the phrase, **"*Niente E Imposibile*"** (Nothing is Impossible!) – a principle my mother lived by all her life. I guess his mother believed it too.

Rome was an especially enchanting city with so many monuments all lit up at night. One that seemed to loom over us wherever we went was the National Monument to **King Vittorio Emanuele II** which also housed the Tomb of the Unknown Italian Soldier. Every road seemed to connect to the sprawling and very busy roundabout (as traffic rotaries were called) which surrounded this striking focal point in Rome known as **The Wedding Cake**. It was easy to see how the monument received its nickname. Almost five hundred feet wide and two hundred feet high, three levels of white marble tiers are elaborately adorned with exterior staircases, Corinthian columns, and numerous statues. We always knew where we were when we saw Victor Emmanuel.

Soon, we were about to say "***Arrivederci Roma***" when we arrived at the train station with just moments to spare. My mother INSISTED on jumping into a taxi in the POURING RAIN so that we could go to the Fountain of Trevi and throw in our coins. According to the legend as she told it, you must turn around and throw them in backwards just like in the movies. If you do, you will return to Rome. She wasn't going to take a chance. Her Irish superstition kicked in at times – a backup plan in case The Fund needed some help. It took us about ten minutes to arrive and another five to convince the taxi driver to stay there and wait for us. With lots of gestures and an important word in our new Italian vocabulary (***ASPETTA!* WAIT!***)*, we finally got our point across.

Keep in mind, this was not some insignificant fountain among the 1400 plus water features found in Rome. Measuring about 100 feet high and 150 feet across, it was immense – a massive monument considered to be one of the most stunning in the entire world! It has been featured in many films over the years – perhaps the most notable being Federico Fellini's ***La Dolce Vita*** (The Sweet Life). At least we didn't jump into the fountain with our clothes like Anita Ekberg and Marcello Mastroianni, but we were probably just as wet. We were drenched by the torrential rain and engulfed by the dense mist emanating from the water gushing out of hundreds of spouts. We climbed down several slippery terraces to the water level, turned around backwards, and threw in our coins. Was it those coins or The Fund? I'm not superstitious, but we returned to Rome – many times!

Somehow, we managed to visit London before we returned to the states. It was all very proper, and we enjoyed being pampered. Mom and The Doctor went out to eat while my sister and I dined in the room. A traditional butler ushered in a formal serving table with delicious lamb chops under high silver domes. "The Lion Sleeps Tonight" ("In the jungle, the mighty jungle, the lion sleeps tonight") was popular and seemed to play over and over. In 1961, it became a number one hit in the United States with the best-known version by the doo-wop group, the Tokens…"a-weema-weh, a-weema-weh, a-weema-weh, a-weema-weh." We couldn't leave London without seeing Big Ben, the clock tower which looms over Westminster Palace, and my mother made sure we learned to pronounce the River Thames (tems).

Soon we were on our way home after such an enlightening experience. My mother knew it would be a priceless opportunity for her girls. She didn't hesitate to act. She grabbed hold of it and didn't let go. The impact of the trip lasted throughout our lives. We learned to love and appreciate people from diverse backgrounds and walks of life at an early age – especially beneficial during the formative years. It shaped our perspective in life and created a desire to continually travel and see the wonders of the world.

By the way, the rest of the story is – we don't know whatever happened with Bingo.

The Spanish Steps in Rome at the top of Via Condotti – the Rodeo Drive of Rome

The three fashionistas

Michelangelo's Moses in Rome

Victor Emmanuel II National Monument

The Fountain of Trevi in Rome

London

Chapter Three

"3 B'S AND A CON MAN"

(THE BEACH, THE BERKSHIRES, BOSTON)

Other memorable trips throughout the late fifties and early sixties were closer to home. We often went to New York City to see the Rockettes kick up their long legs in precise synchrony at Rockefeller Center. My sister and I skated while Mom and The Doctor dined inside at one of the upscale restaurants overlooking the famous rink. At night, we'd go to the Copacabana Nightclub and the 21 Club. The big band/supper clubs were in their glory. We'd eat dinner in elegant surroundings, and Mom and The Doctor would dance the night away. During February school vacations, we'd always go somewhere for a week – Atlantic City or Montreal (too cold – we got on a train and came right back). However, one adventure presented a new challenge none of us had ever encountered in life. It left its mark until this day.

We had a beautiful beach house at the Connecticut Shore. Was it because of The Fund? Possibly. It was a two-story, five-bedroom, two-bath, winterized home just a few hundred yards from the water! On the last day of school every year, my mother would pick us up in our 1957 silver Chevy station wagon packed with everything we would need for the entire summer. We didn't even go home. We just picked up my grandmother, started our drive to Giant's Neck, and always stopped at Harry's Place in Colchester – an outside drive-in with umbrella-shaded picnic tables. They're actually listed on the National Register of Historic Places but were more famous for the most delicious hamburgers we've ever had.

Harry's Place in Colchester, Connecticut

Our beach house at Giant's Neck in East Lyme, Connecticut

Nanny, Mom, and Aunt Helen

We loved the beach! We didn't realize how privileged we were to be able to spend the ENTIRE SUMMER on the ocean. In fact, we would buy our new school clothes on Labor Day Weekend down the road in New London. That's how long we stayed at the beach. My grandmother, whom we called Nanny, watched us while my mother returned to work at the clinic (the Furcolo Clinic) at least three days a week. I don't know how she did it.

At the time, we didn't appreciate how many sacrifices she made to provide so much for us. She drove almost 90 minutes each way, cooked dinner when she came back, and entertained tons of guests when The Doctor and my grandfather came down on the weekends. My grandmother cooked occasionally until one of the local fishermen left our regular order of live lobsters loose in the refrigerator. We always left our doors unlocked. We must have been at the beach when he arrived. When we returned after a full day on the shore, Nanny opened the refrigerator door, and the lobsters all tumbled out and frantically crawled everywhere! She screamed at the top of her lungs and was done with cooking after that.

There was a clubhouse right behind our cottage. We went there every morning to sing songs like "John Brown's Baby Had A Cold Upon His Chest," to play games like "Red Rover, Red Rover," and to do crafts like braiding lanyards out of gimp. I wasn't crazy about the activities, but at 11 a.m. we all walked to the beach for our swimming lessons. Learning to swim in the ocean at an early age was one of the best things that ever happened to us. To this day, I can float or tread water for hours without touching the bottom. I was afraid the little crabs would bite my toes, so I never put my feet down. Plus, we had to force ourselves to jump into the ice-cold early-morning ocean water for our class. I think of that every time I need to face some difficult challenge in life. I just "jump in" knowing the shock to the body and mind will be brief. I grew to love swimming and the ocean, but I don't swim anymore. I'm scared of Jaws (and chlorine)!

After lunch, we walked back to the beach and Nanny stayed there with us all day. She would dog paddle (the only stroke she knew) all the way to a nearby island. She had to cross a channel where all the boats came in. Everyone was afraid for her, but she loved it. My sister and I put iodine in baby oil to get really tan. We just got really sunburned, and Nanny had to rub Noxzema all over us.

Nanny was quite a character. When we were at home, she took us to the movies every week - often to see the latest Marilyn Monroe films. We'd take the bus downtown, shop in the big department stores, and buy chocolate eclairs on the way home. She went to all the funerals and made my sister pinch the deceased just to make sure they were really gone. Nanny was very outspoken at times and had the funniest expressions: "Here's your hat, what's your hurry?" or "The things you see when you don't have a gun!" To this day, we still love the movies. I won't sit near anyone when I go. I love to lose myself and be completely engulfed by the big screen.

When we weren't sunbathing, my sister, Nora, would swim out to the raft with the big kids. I collected different varieties of seaweed that had been abandoned by the ebb tide on the sandbars – fuzzy brown strands, shiny green lettuce-like leaves, red slabs that looked like leather - and pretended I had a fish market on the big, flat rocks. We gathered mussels, cracked them, and tied them to a string to use as bait to go crabbing. We'd keep all the crabs in a pail and then dump them out at the end of the day.

At other times we'd step very carefully over GIANT horseshoe crabs so that we could go clamming. They looked like they were from the dinosaur age with hard, round shells almost two feet long, a tail that looked like a spear, and underneath, ten legs (claws?)! It was like navigating through a minefield yet well worth it because clamming was really neat. We just walked on the sandbar in knee-deep water and felt for the hard, round clams with the bottoms of our feet. When we stepped on one, it would dig down so fast. You had to be quick to catch them. We kept the clams because my mother and grandfather loved steamers. Ugh! They were the only ones who ate them.

Every Sunday we went to church in Soundview – another beach where the Italian community from home rented cottages by the week. We were often late to everything, so we had to listen to the Mass with the crowds on the outside steps of the church. Standing room only! We didn't mind. We could get out faster. We would go late, leave early, and the whole event was just about 20 minutes. Perfect! Onward to blueberry pancakes at Black Point Beach down the road.

The weekends were great at the beach. Cocktail parties were very fashionable at the time, and Mom and The Doctor went to all of them. My sister went to dances at the clubhouse while my little friends and I would sit on the outside steps in the dark and watch them through the screen doors. They would dance to Pat Boone's "April Love," Paul Anka's "Put Your Head on My Shoulder," and the best one of all – "Sleep Walk." Friends and relatives came down from Springfield, and at night they would all play poker around the kitchen table. We had a large kitchen which became larger because my mother "removed" the back stairway. **She was very handy with a crowbar**. She merely had to start projects. Then someone HAD to come in to finish them.

Among our frequent guests at the beach was a couple named Mr. and Mrs. Carson. He was a tax consultant of some sort. They drove down most weekends throughout the summer. She always brought scalloped potatoes with ham. That's the main thing we remember about her. We really enjoyed their company. They were so funny and accommodating. They'd take my sister and me wherever we needed to go. We really didn't know them before. Suddenly, they were in our lives, but that wasn't unusual. The Doctor always had friends coming and going.

Soon, the summer ended as it did every year, and we went back home. The cooler temperatures brought in the fall, and we headed to The Berkshires. It was a very popular area for New Yorkers who wanted to get out of the city and see the fall foliage in the hills of Massachusetts. We went up every weekend, but it wasn't for the leaves. The Doctor was involved in some sort of arrangement to buy a racetrack! It would be called Berkshire Downs. It was quite a story which ended up on the front page of our local Springfield Union Newspaper with **MY MOTHER BEING SUED WITH FRANK SINATRA AND DEAN MARTIN!**

Opening Day at Berkshire Downs in September, 1960

The Doctor and Dario at Berkshire Downs

What I remember most about Berkshire Downs in the early stages is walking through a lot of mud to get to a dining room in the grandstand where very gracious waiters served lunch and took our bets while we watched the races. I think we were under the age limit to gain access to gambling venues, but we were with The Doctor. It was no problem. My mother wasn't a gambler although she did like the stock market a lot. She kept and enlarged The Fund by means of it. When it came to horse races, she only bet on gray horses - $2.00 at the most - and was satisfied to just get her money back from the day's outing. She often tried to teach me how to read the handicapping cards with the betting picks. They explained which horses came from good racing stock, which ones ran well in the mud, and so on. She didn't pay attention to the details. She just liked gray horses. Sometimes they won.

When we weren't in the Berkshires on the weekends, we had wonderful parties at our home. Some of the guests were "associates" from the racetrack along with local judges appointed by the Doctor's son (the Governor of Massachusetts). We loved to entertain! We'd put a door over the kitchen table so that my grandfather could tend the "bar" all night. My mother cooked tons of food – hams, turkeys, lasagna with the tiny meatballs inside (the way the Italian patients at the clinic taught her), and Easter Pizza. They call it Pizza Rustica in the cookbooks. Wrapped in a thick, bread-like pastry crust, it was filled with salami, capicola, hot and sweet pepperoni, ricotta and **Caciocavallo** cheese ("cheese on horseback"), a Southern Italian specialty. I knew there was some connection with horses. Mom made it on a huge sheet pan and then, very skillfully, turned it upside down halfway through the baking process so that the oil from all the fatty meats dripped out. It was delicious – served warm right out of the oven or as a cold treat for breakfast. At the parties, we always had music playing from the *Rome Adventure* and *Never on Sunday* albums.

We served everything in our formal dining room. Just like the kitchen at our beach house, the dining room was enhanced by my mother's handiwork with the crowbar. It was amazing what she could accomplish by just clawing a wall. This time, she removed the adjoining pantry to extend the dining room. My mother decorated the new space with Chelsea Bird Waverly wallpaper over white wainscoting. It had trailing vines and tree branches dotted with blue and red birds. Everything else in the room had blue accents. My mother loved everything blue – especially Wedgewood and cobalt. The dining room had a large picture window which overlooked a huge stone terrace and five acres of land right in the middle of the city – most of it cultivated by The Doctor's Italian patients.

My grandfather also had a huge garden in our yard. As the summer progressed, he went to garden shops and purchased fully grown vegetable plants – cukes, tomatoes, peppers, and zucchini – and spread them throughout his garden. Grandpa told everyone what a good gardener he was because his crop came out so early. One time he found a huge snapping turtle which wandered up to our yard from Johnny Appleseed Park at the end of the road.

Mom was really the one with the green thumb. She planted beautiful varieties of rose bushes all around the house and along the one-hundred-foot frontage. There was always a bleeding-heart plant wherever she lived and multiple beds of deep purple irises and reddish-orange poppies. Whenever we drove to the beach on the old roads through the town of Flanders, Connecticut, Mom recited the poem, "In Flanders Fields" (the poppies blow), a sad war poem from World War I.

Mom refinished an elegant breakfront where she displayed a special and unique set of formal dinnerware. She always told us that the pattern was created for the Duke of Windsor who abdicated the throne to marry for love. Supposedly the pattern was discontinued - perhaps because of the scandal. At any rate, we only looked at the dishes. Maybe we used them once or twice for very special occasions. There was another set of white dishes with a wide cobalt blue border and a gold design in the middle – very elegant. The rest of the time, we just used Lenox or Royal Worcester. We were spoiled! Even today, I still enjoy dining in such elegant surroundings with linen tablecloths and fresh flowers. It's my favorite pastime.

Mom's poppies

Grandpa's snapping turtle

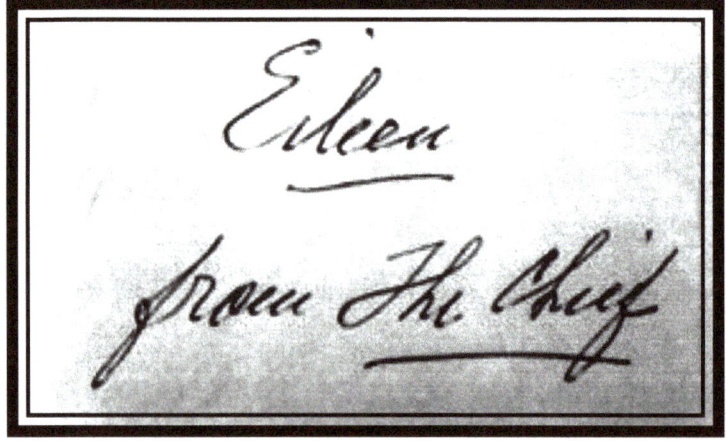

A note from The Doctor to Mom

One very memorable feature at every party was my mother's recital of lengthy, narrative poems or celebrated speeches. Her repertoire included "Dan McGrew" (whose "poke was pinched by the lady known as Lou), "The Highwayman" (a barkeeper's daughter kills herself to warn her lover and save his life), and "The Face on the Barroom Floor" (an artist loses his lover to another man, turns to drink, sketches her face on the barroom floor and falls over dead before he can finish). Wow, really? Kind of morbid.

There was a favorite that we all loved. As soon as the guests started "feeling good" as my mother would say, they would shout, "do 'Gunga Din!'" Without hesitation, she would stand up and "perform" the piece. Articulated in the Cockney accent that British soldiers would have used while serving on the frontier of India, she drove home the harsh berating of the loyal water carrier in each chorus and then brought us to tears when she delivered – very dramatically - the solemn final line,

"You're a better man than I am, Gunga Din."

The lowly water carrier had risked his own life to save the heartless officer and to give him one last drink of water. In doing so, he took a bullet and died on the battlefield hoping he had pleased his master well. It was a quote we used over and over throughout our lives whenever we wanted to express genuine admiration for someone who denied himself for others in an extraordinary way.

Another favorite was Spartacus' famous speech. You would have thought it was Kirk Douglas himself rallying his fellow enslaved gladiators to revolt against Rome. The Doctor loved the beginning and often signed notes to us "From The Chief."

SPARTACUS: *Ye call me chief; and ye do well to call him chief who for twelve long years has met upon the arena every shape of man or beast the broad Empire of Rome could furnish, and who never yet lowered his arm.*

When you have a chance, glance at the full version of these pieces on the last pages of this memoir. Notice the length! My mother **RECITED THEM BY HEART** and there wasn't a dry eye in the place. Who does that?

Mom often tried to interest us in public speaking by sending us to Elocution Classes. The "teacher" lived downtown in a railroad style apartment on the fourth floor. Her name was Althea Delight Clark. The epitome of etiquette and grace, Miss Clark always greeted us with perfect posture, a classic Pendleton suit, and matching pumps. Most of the time she taught the local lawyers how to present powerful arguments in court. I was in a small group of three. One of my classmates was Susan Breck, the daughter of the historic Breck Shampoo Company which originated in our city. Her family probably felt that poise and elegance were important qualities to cultivate. Mom's goal was to "break me out of my shell." I was very shy and always hid behind my mother when she tried to introduce me to people. Thankfully (or not?), she said Miss Clark shattered that shell because I never stopped talking after taking those classes.

We learned proper enunciation by practicing rhymes like:

Mr. Knox kept his socks in a brown and orange polka-dotted box.
Park (Pahk) your car (cah) in the Harvard Yard.
How do you do, goose? Are you a new (nyuu) goose? Quite new, are you?

We had to march up and down the long hallway balancing books on our heads or lie on the floor and raise the same books with our diaphragms while we breathed PROPERLY. It's a lost art! I learned to recite the Gettysburg Address which is engraved on the walls of the Lincoln Memorial. I only remember the first two lines:

Four score and seven years ago our fathers brought forth on this continent, a new nation, conceived in Liberty, and dedicated to the proposition that all men are created equal...

I wish I remembered more. I really liked it, but I didn't like public speaking. Whenever my mother asked me to recite a piece or play the piano, I flat out refused, stomped up the stairs, and slammed my bedroom door! So much for entertaining the guests. My sister also had her rebellious moments. Whenever she resisted, my mother would recite a nursery rhyme by Henry Wadsworth Longfellow:

> There was a little girl,
> Who had a little curl,
> Right in the middle of her forehead.
> When she was good,
> She was very, very good,
> But when she was bad, she was horrid.

Then Mom would tell Nora, "That's you!" We knew she was kidding (sort of).

Speaking of the piano, my sister became a very accomplished pianist. After the home lessons with Mrs. Tesoro, she attended the Conservatory of Music and learned how to play a very difficult piece – "Rhapsody in Blue" by George Gershwin. She practiced for hours and days and months. The composition became famous when it ushered in the Jazz Age in 1924 because it was the first to integrate jazz rhythms with classical music. It was known for "emotional exuberance, wildness, and magnificence" as it moved through changing keys, tempos, and themes – always returning to a beautiful, haunting melody. If you don't believe me, just listen to Leonard Bernstein's rendition of it with the New York Philharmonic in 1976 (on YouTube) **– all 17 minutes of it!**

Sadly, we had a fire in our home soon after, and the piano strings melted! That was the end of the piano lessons.

More sacrifices! How much did my mother deny herself to pay for all of those lessons? No doubt, she withdrew from The Fund to make it all possible. Why didn't we think about it until long after she was gone? Having no concept of the planning, improvising, and doing whatever was necessary to give us such a well-rounded foundation, we just took it all for granted.

Piano lessons

Nora (far right) at the Conservatory of Music

3 B'S AND A CON MAN   65

Clearly, our parties were memorable. During the period of Berkshire Downs, the guests became household names. We didn't have a clue that they would eventually fill the pages of newspaper records, court transcripts, and FBI files! We were like the kids in *The Sopranos* who naively believed their father was really a waste-management consultant. That's not to say that The Doctor was part of the "underworld." I don't think he was, at all. His life merely intersected, possibly, with politics and organized crime like a Venn diagram. As one article put it, the **"Furcolo crowd mobbed up!"**

So, here's the story that was told in the media – a story which according to one reporter – "had everything: corruption, organized crime, Hollywood stars, a religious sect, politics, legal battles…and more court dates than race dates."

The Doctor had a lot of "hobbies." His first love was architecture, and he designed and built many beautiful and unique homes – more about that later. He was also intrigued by new business ventures, and in the early sixties, one presented itself – an interest in a racetrack. Evidently, only two racetracks in Massachusetts met the location regulations issued by the MA Gaming Commission: Suffolk Downs in East Boston and the Hancock Raceway in the Berkshires. Suffolk Downs was well-established, but interested parties wanted to convert Hancock's fairground harness track into a real commercial enterprise. They would call it Berkshire Downs.

Investors were needed to construct a proper grandstand with general seating for 3,000 fans, 500 box seats, a restaurant, a gentlemen's bar, and a cocktail lounge. It was estimated that 10,000 people would fit into the compound when completed. A man named B. A. Dario, the owner of the Lincoln Downs Racetrack in Rhode Island, stepped up to provide some of the funds. Since he was from the Providence area, speculation ran high that he was representing Raymond Patriarca, "***Il Patrone***," the alleged longtime boss of the Patriarca Crime Family whose control extended throughout New England for more than three decades. Dario denied knowing any of the parties involved.

Another problem – the Gaming Commission only issued a certain number of racing days per year and most of those usually went to Suffolk Downs. Was the fact that The Doctor's son was Governor have any bearing on the matter? Maybe it was just a coincidence, but soon after The Doctor entered the picture, Berkshire Downs got its dates!

The Shakers also tried to block the proposal. They were very conservative and declared that gambling and drinking were the Devil's work. An informant later testified that a substantial contribution was made to a religious group. Suddenly, all systems "were go" for Berkshire Downs.

According to witnesses who later testified, The Doctor didn't want his name to appear on any documents in order to avoid association with his son, the Governor. So, he put his interests (stock and cash) in his tax consultant's name – you guessed it – Mr. Carson, our "new friend" from the beach. He also put more shares in my mother's name which is why she was later sued with Frank Sinatra and Dean Martin (on the front page of our local newspaper). Both stars became major shareholders and were put on the Board of Directors. People wondered if they were a front for the Mob. Frank Sinatra later testified that he had no idea a "reputed mafia don" was involved and withdrew his $55,000 investment when they named him vice-president "without his knowledge." Mr. Patriarca (***Il Patrone***) testified that he never met the man (Frank Sinatra)! The lawsuit involving my mother and the Hollywood stars resulted when the former owner of the Hancock Raceway at the fairgrounds sued them. He claimed he was "forced" to sell his property because interested parties had political influence over the State Racing Commission. The new owners denied the pressure. It's an "absolute fabrication!" The case was settled out of court.

Suddenly, everything blew up. That's where Boston came into the picture. Boston is beautiful. It's a wonderful walking city. There are manicured public gardens with swan boats, a historic harbor of Boston Tea Party fame, posh Newbury Street for shoppers, the North End Italian community, and world class restaurants! We went to most of them. If you ask me, that's the best way to study history! Ye Olde Union Oyster House, Boston's oldest restaurant (1826), was supposedly frequented by the Kennedys. Another one, Faneuil (rhymes with Samuel) Hall's Durgin-Park (1827) had communal tables served by big, strong women with a gruff approach. They featured massive slabs of prime rib, Boston Baked Beans, and warm, homemade Indian Pudding made with cornmeal, molasses, and vanilla ice cream dripping down over the whole thing. My sister's favorite!

We also frequented Jacob Wirth (1868), Locke-Ober (1875), and most of all, the Maliave (1885). We went to them all on a regular basis! Parker's Restaurant in the Parker House Hotel

(1855) created Boston Cream Pie and Parker House Rolls and introduced Bostonians to a French menu of turtle soup, oysters, and goose. We stuck with the Boston Cream Pie and Boston Schrod.

We often stayed at the Parker House overnight because of its proximity to – of all things – the **courthouse!** Mom and The Doctor went there daily while my sister and I walked around the corner to Washington Street and amused ourselves with the bargains in Filene's Basement (and sub-basement). We learned how to try on clothes in the aisles like all experienced shoppers.

My sister introduced me to the finer things in life like shopping, art, decorating, and the cha-cha! After Filene's Basement, we always went to the Isabella Stuart Gardner Museum. It was designed to resemble a Venetian palace with a beautiful two-story courtyard and bright orange nasturtiums cascading down from open stone-encased windows twenty feet above. We went there several times and just wandered around soaking up the ambiance. It has one of the world's most noteworthy art collections. I don't think we ever looked at the paintings. It's a shame because the museum later became the site of the **world's largest art heist**!

> In the early morning hours after St. Patrick's Day in 1990, two thieves disguised as police officers talked their way into the museum, tied up two guards, and removed the masterpieces from their frames. Among the 13 pieces are three by Rembrandt, including his only seascape, "The Storm on the Sea of Galilee," "A Lady and Gentleman in Black," and a stamp-sized self-portrait; Flinck's "Landscape with an Obelisk"; Degas' sketches; "Chez Tortoni" by Manet; an ancient Chinese vase; and a bronze finial eagle from atop a Napoleonic flag.

In spite of a ten-million-dollar reward, none of the works have been recovered! To this day, empty frames remain on the walls in hope of the time when the precious pieces of art return to their home.

We also stayed at The Copley Plaza Hotel (now The Fairmont Copley Plaza). It's a majestic place with huge marble columns two stories high, gold gilt woodwork everywhere, elaborately sculpted ceilings, and the largest fresh floral arrangements I've ever seen – at least three feet across. I still go there today just to sit in their lobby and pretend it's my living room.

We stayed at The Copley Plaza in Back Bay because it's directly across from the Boston Public Library (the first "large, free, municipal, lending library in the United States") and right around the corner from Café Budapest. (Food always enters the picture.) The library was important. That's where my mother discovered Mr. Carson's real name and finally cracked the case. Like **Albert Einstein once said**, **"The only thing that you absolutely have to know, is the location of the library."** (Of course, that was before the Internet.)

So, the case…

At some point in this long saga, Mr. Carson decided he wanted to keep The Doctor's investment that had been put in his name! The money, the stock - he claimed it all belonged to him, that he was a major investor in the track. As one reporter put it, "He turned the tables on Dr. Furcolo, sold the stock, bought a bond, hid it under his rug, and blew the rest at a racetrack in Florida." Mr. Carson's lawyer implied that the temptation was too great. **Having all the shares in his name, "he was like a man who gets too much change at the supermarket."**

The first case was tried in Suffolk County Court in downtown Boston. That's why we were there for days and weeks at a time. It was a civil suit over the ownership of the stock. No determination was made, and the Judge threw the case out of court invoking the doctrine of "unclean hands."

The real action took place at home in Hampden Superior Court since Mr. Carson lived in Springfield like us. The Commonwealth accused Mr. Charles Carson of the larceny of a promissory note, voting shares of stock, and non-voting shares – all totaling about $200,000. It was a considerable sum. Don't forget inflation. **The value of $200,000 in the early sixties had the buying power of almost $2,000,000 today!**

Mr. Carson testified that he was given the money and the stock for patching up an argument between Mom and The Doctor! He said The Doctor made him an equal partner (never happened)! Mr. Carson's lawyer described him as a "loyal friend wishing only to see his rightful interest in the stock." Many witnesses including a "parade of judges" confirmed that, as far as they knew, everything belonged to The Doctor. What was the truth? A jury of ten men and two women had to decide. By the way, it only took them two hours!

Remember the library? My mother's research revealed that Mr. Carson's real name was really Charles Gershanovitch (or something similar) and that he had a sketchy past. During the trial we ate dinner out every night at our favorite local Italian places. **Hold on – this is not about food.** All the Italian restaurants in our area were run by people from Naples in Southern Italy like the Doctor. Somehow, they all settled here. This meant that they were Neapolitan or "*Napolitano paisanos*" – comrades – with a bond of loyalty to one another. Of course, it didn't hurt that The Doctor was also their beloved physician.

One night during the trial, we went to Happyland, a restaurant owned by a short, robust Italian woman named Grace Nardi. She may have been the one who originally introduced the infamous accountant, Mr. Carson, to The Doctor. Somehow it all came out that he had conned her family too. Whatever went down, he blackmailed them, threatening to cause her son's fiancée or maybe her niece (the details are vague) to be deported back to Italy!

So, the next day in court, my mother thought of Grace Nardi. She was worried about the portrayal of Mr. Carson as an "innocent man who just wanted his fair share." Convinced that she could demonstrate a pattern, Mom moved fast!

She got on the phone and shouted, "Grace, whatever you're doing, put on your coat and go outside. I'll have a cruiser pick you up in two minutes!"

Grace Nardi exclaimed, "I'm in the kitchen cooking lunch for the restaurant!"

"The Doctor needs you now! You have to tell your story to the jury."

Grace immediately threw her coat over her apron, went outside, and jumped in the cruiser. (My mother and The Doctor seemed to have ways of arranging things like that – cruisers, sheriffs, etc.)

In less than 15 minutes, an out of breath Grace Nardi boldly marched down the center aisle of the courtroom and climbed right up into the witness box – coat, apron, and all. **In her heavy Italian accent and broken English, she delivered an explosive, Oscar winning, riveting account of everything that "sonofabitch" did.**

> Verdict: Guilty on all counts of "Greed Inspired Larceny!"
> Sentence: Two years for each of three indictments (served simultaneously):
> Larceny of capital stock
> Larceny of a promissory note
> Larceny of money proceeds from the sale of stock

Mr. Carson was ordered to begin his sentence immediately despite his lawyer's claim that he had a bad heart (more like a wicked heart). When he was asked to produce the $200,000 bond that had been hidden under his rug, Mr. Carson said he couldn't find it! **The Doctor never recovered any of his investment.**

"All's well that ends well." Or is it? Losing the money wasn't the worst of it. When you're taken in by a "confidence man," you never really recover. You start to question your sense of judgement – how well you read people. The Doctor was never really the same after that. The ordeal "took the wind out of his sails" as they say. That's what Mr. Carson, a real con man, did to all of us.

At least it made a great story to tell at dinner over the years. The reporter covering the trial concluded, **"Forget Seabiscuit. They should make a movie out of this mess!"** Who would play the role of Mom? Katherine Hepburn? Grace Kelly? They had Mom's beauty and resolve.

Ye Olde Union Oyster House Restaurant

The Swan Boats in Boston

The Isabella Stuart Gardner Museum

The Fairmont Copley Plaza Hotel

The Boston Public Library

Mom and Nora

Chapter Four

"RAHAR'S INN"

It wasn't long – maybe a few months – and another prospect materialized. My mother always said you have to jump on an opportunity when you see it. Otherwise, it will be too late. You'll miss it, and they don't come around that often. She had a lot of practice.

A very famous hotel in Northampton was for sale. According to records from the Massachusetts Historical Commission,

> Rahar's Inn opened in 1897 by Richard Rahar. President Calvin Coolidge lived at Rahar's when he commenced his practice of law in Northampton. It was reported that the safe in the Inn once held the announcement from Peary that he had discovered the North Pole. The Inn was for years a favorite meeting place of Smith College students. (and all the Ivy League men from Dartmouth and Amherst who came to meet them every weekend!)

So, the place had a lot of history. The upper two floors had at least twenty hotel rooms for rent. The first floor had two bars, two dining rooms, a cocktail lounge, a lobby, the cozy Coolidge Room (about four feet by four feet), the round Admiral Peary Room, and the Sophia Smith Room – both about six feet in diameter. All three had beautiful murals painted on the walls from floor to ceiling depicting the theme of each room. They were the perfect size for intimate gatherings. The basement had a Rathskeller called The Elbow Room.

The location was spectacular. It was situated on a small hill only about one hundred feet from the heart of Main Street in Downtown Northampton and only two blocks from Smith College! The hotel had been vacant for years, but Mom and The Doctor were sure they could bring it back to the glory of its heyday.

One drawback was that they had to produce a sizable down payment. Where did they get it? They sold our beautiful beach house for $10,000! Mom was thrilled she could get a mortgage for $150,000 **in her name** – quite an accomplishment for a woman in the sixties. Remember the Elizabeth Cady Stanton quote in the beginning? **"The best protection any woman can have is courage."** I guess my mother had a lot of it. Would you want a mortgage of $1,500,000 (the value today)? A woman on her own with two teenage girls?

So, they bought it, and we began our daily trek on the old road from Springfield to Northampton. Now that the highway is in, you can do it in about thirty minutes. At the time, the only option was the old Route 5 along the Connecticut River. It wouldn't have been bad, but we always transported lots of things in addition to our dog and cat. (We stayed over a lot and couldn't leave them at home.) Also, my mother emptied out a good part of our house to decorate the lobby and other parts of the Inn. We loaded the car with antique furniture, Oriental rugs, decorative items, paintings – you name it, we brought it! Contractors buzzed all around as they worked to restore the place. I don't know how my mother found the energy!

She had two friends who had been patients at the Clinic - a "couple" named Harry and Fredette. We called him Fredett**ie**. They LOVED to decorate and had a flair for it. They had three big, beautiful homes right next to each other in the historic Hill-McKnight area of our city. Two houses were converted into nursing homes and provided a nice income for them. They had a great system going. They lived right next door, so they could run in and out to care for the residents. When it snowed, they sent them outside to shovel "for exercise." At least that's what they told us. Maybe they were kidding.

Harry and Fredettie loved to entertain. They'd call us up late at night and invite us to go over. Mom and the "boys" and another friend from the Clinic would have martinis and Nora's chocolate cake. We wandered throughout the house and played music in all the living rooms – "Misty" and "Chances Are" by Johnny Mathis and "Autumn Leaves" and "Unforgettable" by Nat King Cole. Decorated to the hilt, the house made us feel like we were in a fancy hotel. We often stayed until 2:00 in the morning or just stayed overnight. We had our choice of bedrooms. Was it summer? I don't remember what happened with school in the mornings.

Harry and Fredettie were the ideal people to help decorate Rahar's. They flitted around back and forth and were quite exuberant when they found the perfect piece for the perfect place. The Doctor wasn't happy about the arrangement. He didn't know what to make of them. It helped that he often drank martinis at the bar in the cocktail lounge and lost track of all the activity.

There was a lot of funny business going on there. The "friendly" bartender was a bit too eager to set a martini in front of The Doctor throughout the afternoons. We later found out that he and the janitor were stealing cases of liquor on a regular basis! We had noticed that the liquor inventory didn't add up. So, late one night, we hid upstairs and spied on them from the windows. Sure enough – they were carrying boxes out the back and loading them into a truck! The waitress was in on it too. All of them had been there together in the past and knew the place inside and out better than us.

The Doctor didn't believe us! He was conned again! An honorable man all his life, he just couldn't fathom the idea of people taking advantage of others. His mind simply wouldn't go there. I guess he reasoned that Mr. Carson's deception at Berkshire Downs was a freak occurrence – a glitch in the natural order of life. We learned a hard lesson - always begin a venture with NEW STAFF MEMBERS!

Once the renovation was complete, my mother made appointments with all the VIPs in town - the Smith College President, the school's administrators, the professors, and the local government officials. She invited them to open houses and complimentary luncheons to see the revitalized Rahar's Inn. Seeing the restoration firsthand would assure them that the Smith women and the local gentry would be in a topnotch establishment. Mom was quite a public relations promoter.

She had attended a Dale Carnegie course which promised courage, confidence, effective speaking, leadership qualities, and memory enhancement. She learned a technique which served me well on examinations all through school. It involved a mnemonic rhyme: one, run; two, zoo; three, tree; four, door; five, hive; six, sticks; seven, heaven; eight, gate; nine, wine; and ten, den. For example, for "five, hive" you picture a word, name, or person flying all around the beehive like little bees. For "ten, den" you picture something coming out of a big lion's den. It actually worked very well. The course helped my mother remember everyone's name which made them feel special. Before long, all the important events in town were held at Rahar's including Alumni Weekends and college graduation celebrations.

We often helped Mom prepare for the large gatherings. There were huge pizza ovens in the basement kitchen where we baked fifty individual casseroles of baked butternut squash blended with homemade applesauce, heavy cream, and sliced almonds on top. People loved them. We had one fantastic chef whom we met at a cafeteria in downtown Springfield – Eddie. His food was so good that my mother hired him to cook at Rahar's on weekends. Decades before anyone ever heard of gorgonzola garlic bread, he spooned globs of blue cheese melted in butter over loaves of thickly sliced rustic Italian bread. I think he invented the concept since no one else thought of it until many years later. We also learned a neat trick from him. When reheating single portions of generous cuts of prime rib, put a large lettuce leaf over the top of each slice to prevent it from drying out. Eddie was such a great chef and never minded having us around when he prepared his culinary delights.

Of course, the real action was on the weekend nights when we relaxed our constraints a bit. We had three bands at a time – two in the dining rooms on the main floor and another in The Elbow Room downstairs. Mom figured out that the bands would audition for free, so she was able to have three going all at once. It was wild! The Doctor got into his head that "singles" created difficulties, so he only allowed young people on dates to come in. My mother met that challenge. On busy Saturday nights, she stood at the door, explained the dilemma, and paired up the singles. No problem!

The Elbow Room in the Rathskeller was especially exciting when Charles was there. He was a close childhood friend who was like a family member. He and his parents were always with us for holidays, beach outings, and every special event throughout our lives. Charles used to drive my mother crazy because he would take apart every small appliance in our home and line up the parts in some sort of order. He was quite intelligent and just wanted to see how things worked. I don't think he ever put anything back together.

By the time of Rahar's, he was in college and his band often played in the Elbow Room on weekends. We all loved the music of Ray Charles - especially his first top 10 hit, "What'd I Say." Our friend, Charles, played the sax to that song over and over. "Wooly Bully" by Sam the Sham & the Pharaohs had just come out and we all buzzed around humming the chorus: Wooly Bully, Wooly Bully, Wooly Bully...

Whenever my mother walked into the Elbow Room, the music instantly stopped! With a quick signal to the band, Charles immediately switched to Ray Charles' "Hardhearted Hannah" – his tribute to my mother whom he affectionately called "Hardhearted Eileen." It was his term of endearment for her and always brought a beautiful Irish smile to her face. Charles remained a "son" throughout my mother's life. After his parents died (too early), she was like his second mother. He regularly drove over two hours each way to visit her several times a year and always stayed for two or three days at a time. We all looked forward to our leisurely dinners together listening to my mother's stories over and over.

Rahar's Inn in Northampton, Massachusetts

Rahar's Inn today

Nora and Charles

Charlene, Charles, and Nora

Hardhearted Hannah

They call her hardhearted Hannah
The vamp of Savannah
The meanest gal in town
Leather is tough
But Hannah's heart is tougher
She's a gal who likes to see men suffer
To tease 'em and thrill 'em
To torture and kill 'em
Is her delight they say
I saw her at the seashore with a great big pan
There was Hannah pouring water on a drowning man
That's hardhearted Hannah, the vamp of Savannah G-A

It was difficult to check IDs at Rahar's, and we didn't want to turn away our regulars from Smith College. Other establishments had the same problem, so they warned one another when the beverage control officers were on the prowl. One hectic Saturday night, I happened to answer the phone. Later, while passing each other at full speed from room to room, I nonchalantly announced, "Mom, the television people are coming. They said they'll be here soon."

"What?" she asked somewhat puzzled. "The television people?"

"I answered the phone, and they said the ABC people are on their way."

"ABC? That's the Alcoholic Beverage Control!!! Hurry up! Check all the rooms with the bands and make sure no one underage is around!!!

Yeah. I thought ABC was the television network. What can I say? I was barely a teenager at the time. It was almost a big problem.

There were other amusing incidents at Rahar's. On Mother's Day, Mom sold her own mother's dinner because we ran out of food for the guests. Nanny chased the chef with a big cast iron frying pan and tried to get it back. Another chef was very temperamental and brandished a big butcher knife to keep people out of the kitchen. Our fierce German Shepherd constantly climbed through a second-floor window onto the roof and barked at patrons coming in the front door. My sister and I met all kinds of young men from the colleges in the area. That was great!

Every now and then, my mother would stand up and throw a drink in The Doctor's face!!! At the bar! In front of everyone! He must have pushed her beyond her limits. He did that at times. He could be unreasonable at inopportune moments when decisions had to be made or action had to be taken – fast!

It's a VERY DRAMATIC gesture. You stand up abruptly, take the martini, hurl the contents directly into the face, put the glass down, and walk out! No words. (Did I describe it too well? That's because I tried it once - in Boston's Café Budapest accompanied by Hungarian Gypsy violinists. Not something I'm proud of. It just seemed like the natural thing to do at the time.) It helps if the recipients are gentlemen. They just pick up a linen napkin and dab away.

All in all, Rahar's was a great experience, but it was a HUGE operation. The Doctor was not always agreeable to Mom's ideas. He couldn't get used to the fact that she was an equal partner in the venture. Soon, it became a burden. My sister and I were too young or too distracted to help my mother really run the place. I was a young teen, and Nora was in college. Eventually, a decision was made to sell the property to Northampton Community College. In hindsight, it was a shame. Today, that historic landmark is untouchable.

Some sort of problem developed in connection with the closing. My mother received a phone call from a good friend well-known in financial circles. He exclaimed, "Get up to Northampton immediately or you're going to lose everything!" Remember, she had put all the proceeds from the beach house into the property and held what constituted a million-dollar mortgage in her name. The details are vague. That's what happens when you don't ask questions AND MAKE NOTES while all the parties are still alive (despite the many times the stories are told). Once again, she moved fast. She got into her car and flew up to Northampton – just in time! Hopefully, my mother got her $10,000 investment back from the sale of the beach house. Otherwise, the Fund would have been depleted for a long time.

Many years later, we took a drive to Giant's Neck to see the old beach house again. We talked to a neighbor who was raking the grass next door. "We owned this house about forty years ago," we told him.

"Really? It just sold for $975,000!"

My mother always said she regretted selling the properties she acquired over the years – the beach house, my grandmother's house (where Mom collected rent once a week), our own house, a historic townhouse on Mattoon Street, and the Furcolo Clinic (yes, she bought that too!). Those undertakings were a lot to oversee for a woman on her own and in a climate that was not conducive to female entrepreneurs. We could have been millionaires if she held on to them, but we would have missed out on a lot of extraordinary adventures.

My mother was grateful to her friend who saved the day during the sale of Rahar's Inn. She felt indebted to him, so she didn't hesitate when she received a frantic call from him a few years later. He said his family forced him into a nursing home to steal his money. He was a wealthy man, and he was desperate.

"You've got to get me out of here!" he pleaded.

She never backed down from a challenge. It was a real covert operation. Mom put on her white nurse's cap and uniform and parked the car by the side entrance. She entered very casually, acted like she owned the place, and stealthily led him down the hall and out the door!

She rescued him! Beside herself with excitement, she scrambled into the car and settled him into a motel before anyone realized what had happened. Talk about Hollywood thrillers! There was just one problem. He called his family and told them where he was! I guess he forgot they were trying to "get him and his money." Maybe he needed the nursing home after all.

No good deed goes unpunished - or something along that line. My mother was worried about possible consequences, so she enrolled in a hotel-management school and fled to Washington D.C. during a very critical time in our lives. We stayed home alone.

Fritz terrorized the customers at Rahar's

Commercial College To Buy Famed Inn

A buy and sell agreement was signed yesterday by the present owners of Rahar's Inn on Old South St. and Richard D. Pickett, president of Northampton Commercial College. Owners Dr. Charles L. Furcolo of Hampden (father of former Governor Foster Furcolo) and Mrs. Eileen Kane of Springfield agreed to transfer title for an unspecified sum to the local commercial college on or before Sept. 1. Dr. Furcolo and Mrs. Kane purchased the local landmark from the federal government in April of last year. It had been taken by the government in lieu of payment of taxes. According to Mr. Pickett, the inn, well-known to thousands of former area college students, will become a men's dormitory, dining commons and conference center for commercial educational groups. A part of the old inn, now closed for the summer, was originally the first city jail. Later a minister added two floors, making it a residence, and built the present brick wall to eliminate the view of an adjacent tavern. In 1897 Richard Rahar opened it as an inn. During his regime it became famous as the site from which word was first released that Peary's expedition had reached the north pole. Visiting celebrities and actors performing at the Academy of Music lived in the old inn. Former U. S. President Calvin Coolidge lived there while studying law and during his first years of legal practice in the city. Other illustrious names included Fritz Kreisler and Sarah Bernhardt. Mr. Pickett stated that the addition of the inn to the commercial college' complex of buildings makes it possible to accept more students for this fall's freshman class.

The sale of Rahar's Inn to Northampton Community College

Our grandmother's house

Our townhouse in the Mattoon Street Historic District

Chapter Five

"SYLVIE"

After Rahar's, life went back to normal for a while – if you can call anything about our lives normal. We always spent the evenings together in the living room - a room we definitely "lived" in. It was a huge space - maybe fifteen by twenty-five feet – somewhat formal but very inviting at the same time. The focal point was a real Persian almost "wall-to-wall" Oriental rug with a floral design in rich shades of plum and burgundy, or should I say *aubergine* - the French word for those deep purple eggplants (sounds so much better in French).

We had a TV mounted up high on one of two built-in bookshelves which framed a beautiful stone fireplace. Next to it was a small pile of logs which we burned every day. The infamous upright was at the other end under a sizable painting of an attractive woman in a bright red evening gown – also playing the piano. There were wingback chairs with great headrests where The Doctor took "forty winks" most evenings before driving home. My mother changed the slipcovers and the curtains every season and constantly moved the furniture around. It always looked new and fresh.

We never quite understood the "showrooms" others had in their homes with plastic covers on the furniture (although we liked the neatness with everything in its place). Our house wasn't exactly like that. My sister and I had the job of cleaning on Saturday mornings while Mom went grocery shopping and ran errands. Our "housework" consisted of blasting the stereo with Barbra Streisand's *People*, Leonard Bernstein's and Steven Sondheim's *West Side Story*, the Ray Charles' *Dedicated to You* album, one of Robert Goulet's signature songs, "On a Clear Day,"

Our home on Cherry Street

and more. We'd sing and dust at the same time. Once, we knocked over an enormous Chinese lamp, and my sister miraculously glued it back together. My mother never knew until we told her years later. That was the beginning of a skill my sister perfected later in life. She meticulously repaired antique porcelain pieces layer by layer until they looked just like new.

So, cleaning was not our forte. We usually just threw things in place frantically when someone was coming over. All clutter was "relocated" (quickly) to the dining room and doors were closed. Unexpected visitors coming to the back door right into the kitchen? We just shoved all the dirty dishes into the washing machine (not a dishwasher - a washer/dryer combo for laundry right in the middle of the kitchen). We always had the newest appliances - a regular dishwasher and a stovetop on an island with ovens on the wall. It sounds ordinary today, but no one had those things back then. And, thanks to my mother's handiwork with the crowbar, our pantry was removed to make more space for a very large dining room.

In spite of her many enterprises, Mom was actually quite domestic. For breakfast, she grilled those tiny loin lamb chops and served them with toast - on school days and all before she went to work! (We do that today for overnight guests and they're flabbergasted! Lamb chops for breakfast? It was normal for us.) She also made the best apple pies EVER from a huge tree in our yard. During the evenings, she ironed all our sheets, pillowcases, and tablecloths! As I've said before, who does that? She had some sort of press from a laundry called a mangle. It was about three feet wide with two gigantic rollers that would flatten linens until they looked brand new. She set it up in the middle of the living room while we watched *Perry Mason* and *Oh! Susannah*. They must have acquired it during one of their many forays to all the commercial auctions in the area.

The Doctor loved those big sales and often purchased HUGE lots of one item. HUNDREDS (no kidding) of cans of paint (all one color) and Colonial Pine Stain lined the shelves in our basement. We had to carefully step over rolled-up Oriental rugs piled on top of each other. Once there was an entire TRUCKLOAD of green bathroom fixtures – bathtubs, sinks, etc. I guess my sister got the "bug" because she gave up her teaching career and went into the auction business.

George and Nora at Genora's Antiques

That's how I lost my childhood braids!

When my mother wasn't ironing, she sat on the couch and brushed my sister's hair while watching TV. Sometimes she would lie on her side with me in front and lightly run her fingers up and down my arms – for hours! I often wake up at night with my arms straight up in the air and find myself running my own fingers up and down. It must be comforting – a subconscious action that I do in my sleep to remind me of our mother and a truly peaceful and secure time in our lives.

Trimming my hair wasn't as pleasant. Scissors in hand, Mom would start on one side, and it would never be even. Then she would cut more off the other side – over and over until I practically jumped out of my skin when I realized that several inches had been removed. My mother on one side and my sister on the other with raised eyebrows that said, "Oh no. What are we going to do now?" That's how I lost my childhood braids!

School projects were always a family affair in the living room. My sister needed one for a science fair, and my mother had an idea (remember, she was a nurse). We got an empty oatmeal box and tapped, tapped, tapped all the different heart rhythms that signified various cardiac disorders. We recorded the sounds, made signs identifying each condition, and people could play each set of heartbeats at the fair. I think she won 1st place! On Saturday afternoons, we played checkers and gin rummy with The Doctor until Mom made some "quick sauce" and pasta. When she didn't cook, we all went out to our favorite restaurants at least three or four times every week.

Lots of things happened in the living room – the most memorable being our frequent sudden plans to drop everything and go to Europe. Every time we got in the mood and opened a bottle of champagne (always poured into hollow-stemmed glasses so that the champagne would keep bubbling), that was it. We started making transatlantic phone calls and off we went! More about that very soon.

During this period, my mother started to work at the YWCA. I was in high school, and the summer of my sophomore year was approaching (1966). I planned to take a special French course with instructors from France. To really get the sense of what happened next, you have to understand how we lived. I always compared our home life to the play, *You Can't Take It With You*. It was about a wacky family with hobbies like building fireworks, collecting snakes, taking ballet lessons, and writing plays that never got published. Everything happens all at once in – you guessed it – the living room. When interesting people came to visit, **they just stayed – forever**. My sister felt that we were more like *My Family and Other Animals* (also known as *The Durrells in Corfu*). The mother, Mrs. Durrell, was spontaneous, eccentric, and adventurous – just like Mom. And, whenever interesting people came to visit, **they often just stayed**.

Mom and Sylvie

So, this may help you imagine how we came to know Sylvie. She was everything FRENCH – blonde, beautiful, cultured, warm, and had the greatest accent you ever heard - ***Oh là là!*** She had just moved into the YWCA to teach the special French class I would soon be attending that summer. At the beginning, I don't think Mom knew she was one of the French instructors directly imported from France. She just liked her and **brought her home to live with us**. Later, we figured out the rest – that she would be one of the teachers in my summer course!

Sylvie became like another daughter, and she remained a "family" member for the rest of our lives. She married a British pilot and settled in the States. We often drove to her home north of Boston and stayed for days. Sylvie always had interesting guests from around the world. We loved it and fit in perfectly! Eventually, Sylvie moved back to France and retired in Provence.

We had lots of fun with Sylvie. She convinced me to ride our bikes to the French class – five miles each way, up and down hills, twice a day! I was in the best shape of my young adult life. During the class, we read **Le Petit Prince** in the original French, converted it into a play, and learned a little more of the language. On the weekends, we had picnics in Forest Park with candelabras, linen tablecloths, crystal wineglasses, and champagne - of course. We played music from the French film, "*a man and a woman*" or from The *Umbrellas of Cherbourg* on our little tape recorders. People walked by and smiled in amusement.

We "broke into" city pools at midnight, and when we got caught, we pretended we were all French and couldn't speak English. The police were mesmerized by Sylvie and just laughed. Our neighbors almost drove off the road when they went by and saw Sylvie cutting our grass in her bikini!

One night during one of our champagne evenings, Sylvie said, "Why don't you come back to France with me when the course ends?"

"Why not?" was my mother's response. She couldn't leave, but she knew it would be an invaluable opportunity for Nora and me. So, she dipped into The Fund, and we were suddenly off to France for a **month-long** whirlwind excursion.

During those years we always flew on Icelandic Airlines. They had roundtrip student fares for $200. The only catch was that you had to fly to **Reykjavík** in Iceland first – no matter where you were going. We were always in a hurry and never stopped to take a dip in the natural geothermic hot springs with temperatures over one hundred degrees! We did buy an Icelandic long-haired pony rug at the airport. Supposedly, they're not killed for their skins. I wonder.

Then we made the long train trek down to Sylvie's home in **Montbéliard, France** – only nine miles from the Swiss border. It was a charming, picturesque city with colorful homes and red tile roofs. Only about 20,000 people lived there in the sixties, and EVERYONE was so cordial and congenial. The "rule" is to greet a close acquaintance on the road with a handshake and a cheek to cheek "kiss." No matter when or where, you always "*faire la bise*" at least once, but often two or four times back and forth from cheek to cheek. It was so civil!

Sylvie's father was a dentist, and his office was right in their home – the chair, the instruments – fascinating! He also loved to garden. Sylvie brought back seeds to grow corn because the only variety they grew was for farm animals. I think they knew something we didn't (it makes you fat!).

Sylvie's parents were away when we arrived, so Sylvie made us a *crêpe* with only fresh herbs and eggs. It was delicious. We made daily stops to the *pâtisserie.* I always ordered "*thé avec citron*" and an exquisite, flaky ***pâtisserie napoléon.*** I'm sure Nora ordered some sort of scrumptious concoction made with "*chocolat.*" Of course, we always brought home a ***baguette*** for the evening meal. People in ***Montbéliard*** shopped daily for dinner. That's how things were done to make sure everything was fresh. Sylvie's home had a refrigerator, but they only kept cereal in it!

We took a day trip through the countryside to ***Besançon*** and ate wild, brown trout from the Doubs River caught just minutes before being served! We spent a weekend in a very small village called ***Serre-les-Sapins*** to visit Sylvie's sister, Marie-Claire, and her husband, Jean-Marc. **They lived in a castle** with incredible panoramic views of the countryside from tall windows with real wooden shutters that we closed at night. It was exciting and a little bit scary to meander through the "house" with all of its rooms and stairways. Marie-Claire made a delicious ***cassoulet*** for dinner – the trademark of French country cuisine.

We had a wonderful time, but before long it was time to say "*à bientôt*" – see you soon or goodbye for now – a salutation we used whenever we were planning to definitely see them again. And, we did - many times throughout our entire lives.

So, my sister and I packed our things and took a LONG train trip with many stops through the Alps, across the border, and down to Rome! Maybe those coins in the Trevi Fountain really worked. This was my sister's third time to Rome. After our first trip, she went on a European tour in college and found this delightful boutique hotel – a "jewel" we would stay in every time we returned to Rome. The Hotel Dinesen was our home away from home ideally located just one block from the Via Veneto where all the action took place in the "Eternal City" – the city that would go on forever!

Father Greco in Rome

The Hotel Dinesen in Rome

We were going down to Rome to visit a family friend - a priest named Father Greco. During the beach and the clinic years (Furcolo Clinic), Mom became friendly with an Italian family who had been The Doctor's patients – Antoinetta, her husband, Antonio, and their two adult children, Norma and Walter. We went to their home every weekend, and Father Greco was always there. We all sat around the kitchen table eating delicious Italian antipasti, talking, laughing, and eventually playing cards for hours. I usually fell asleep on the living room couch.

Walter was a lawyer in town, and his sister, Norma, was the Fashion Coordinator of a large department store along the lines of Macy's. When we went to the beach, she was a walking fashion statement sporting straw hats with oversized brims, bold colors like orange and lime, and large, round Jackie Kennedy sunglasses. Norma was responsible for selecting the apparel for six floors of showrooms and for the fashion shows in Steiger's Tearoom where my sister modeled shirtwaist dresses so popular in the fifties and sixties. In time, Norma became the Fashion Coordinator for Bloomingdales in NYC! She invited us to visit her EXPENSIVE, TINY apartment right on Central Park which she decorated in "black, white, and FAWN" – not beige or brown, she said, but fawn.

During the weekly card games, we became very friendly with Father Greco. We used to kid around with him all the time. He was a priest of the Stigmatine Order who lived in a monastery around the corner from our home. When we walked our "ferocious" German Shepherd, we often popped in – much to the dismay of the other "brothers" who lived there. Fritz was actually quite behaved when he was on a leash. I took him to obedience school, and he won third place on the final examination day. We rarely told people that there were only three dogs in the class, so coming in third was not a huge accomplishment.

It wasn't his fault. He used to get motion sickness in the car, so we always gave him Dramamine before the ride. It made him too groggy to pay attention. One time, without thinking, I had the pills in my hand and took them myself! I'm not quite sure what happened during that class.

In time, Father Greco was transferred to Rome, and that's why we were on the train heading to see him before going home. There were so many stops on the way, and some were overnight. We perfected the skill of **sleeping on benches in the train stations stretched out on top of all our belongings**. Upon arrival, we called Father Greco, took a taxi to The Dinesen, and headed up to the outdoor cafes on the Via Veneto to have "coke with lemon" the way they served it over there – quite refreshing. At night, we'd stroll up and down the paparazzi-lined boulevard and eat gelato.

One evening, my sister and I mingled with the tourists and strolled around the many illuminated fountains and monuments. It was enchanting. Soon, a group of very friendly and very handsome Italian young men approached and tried to talk to us. They only knew one phrase in English which they "chanted" over and over: *Where are you going? Where are you going?* We turned around and smiled, and they responded, *"Where are you going?"*

Maurizio and Piero in Rome

They followed us for a while. It was fun and exciting. Finally, we said, "To the Colosseum." They were quite content to walk with us and we managed to exchange names (***Come si chiama?***). We eventually figured out that we all spoke a little broken French – no Italian for us, no English for them, but our basic school French seemed to work. "Piero" pointed to himself and to my sister and said "***domani***" – one of the few words we knew in Italian – tomorrow! Somehow, we understood that he wanted to meet again. My sister pointed to me and to her and nodded her head to say yes. In other words, she wasn't going anywhere without me! How he indicated that he would bring someone for me, I don't know, but we got the message. The entourage walked us back to The Dinesen and we all said "***ciao***" until the following night.

The next morning, Father Greco arrived bright and early. We began a personal guided tour of ALL THE CHURCHES IN ROME! I guess we couldn't have seen all 900 of them, but we saw a lot - the Basilica of St. Paul Outside the Walls, St. Peter in Chains, the Basilica of St. John Lateran, the Basilica of St. Peter (in the Vatican) – at least three or four each day. I don't think we ever stopped to eat anywhere.

I have to admit – Father Greco knew some cool things about each place – especially the Vatican. Due to the way the dome is constructed, there is a "whispering gallery" which enables one to **WHISPER** in one area and to be heard by another at the opposite end **more than 700 feet away**! We tried it out. Amazing! Apparently, the sound waves travel on the curves of the dome.

After quite a long day, Father Greco dropped us off at The Dinesen with plans to return bright and early the next morning. We scrambled upstairs and changed our clothes just in time to have the front desk call to announce our guests. When we entered the lobby, Piero smiled, stepped aside, and with an open hand he presented an "assortment" of young, handsome men. I was supposed to choose. We managed all of this without speaking the same language!

"***Domani***" brought the same routine – bright and early – lots of churches. We returned moments before Piero arrived. We climbed into his cute little Fiat and went to pick up Maurizio. He had to climb over a very high wall to sneak out of the firehouse barracks. Apparently, he was in some sort of compulsory civilian service in place of joining the military. This was a ritual we followed every night. Pick up Maurizio, explore Rome until the wee hours, try to catch a few hours of sleep, and be ready to meet Father Greco – you guessed it – bright and early!

Piero and Maurizio knew all the exciting and secret sights in Rome. We walked on the beach in Ostia, peered through a keyhole on Aventine Hill to see the entire Eternal City, and ran up and down the steps of the "new colosseum" in the EUR district ("**Esposizione Universale di Roma**" - Rome's Universal Exposition - a residential and business district originally designed as the site of the World's Fair in 1942 which was canceled because of World War II). Sometimes we'd stop in a little café/bar and have a coke with lemon served in the old glass Coca-Cola bottles. We had the most fun in the little Fiat flying through the labyrinth of alleys, the sprawling roundabouts, and the numerous piazzas. There was no traffic on the road at three in the morning! It was like the car chases in the *Pink Panther* movies.

Sometimes we'd catch a few hours in the afternoons for shopping. "**Standa**" was a large department store with many floors and lots of bargains. We bought long cardigan sweaters which almost reached the ground. They hadn't made it to the States yet and we thought the style was very cool and fashionable. We stuffed our bags with them along with tons of skirts and tops that we could model at school when we returned. Somehow, we found a street market and I bought a VERY HEAVY marble bust of a beautiful peasant girl. We never thought about carrying everything home on the airplane.

We were definitely burning the candle at both ends as they say. It all came to a head when we stayed out a little too late one night. The sun had already risen when we reached The Dinesen. We had to **scramble in the front door and go right out the side door** to meet Father Greco! There was no time to go upstairs, change, sleep, eat – nothing.

He was a bit earlier than usual because he had a very special day planned for us. Father Greco was so excited because we were going to attend an audience with **Il Papa**, Pope John XXIII, at his summer residence, **Castel Gandolfo**.

After an hour's drive from Rome, we arrived and found a spot in front of **thousands** of devotees. It was quite a phenomenon – definitely a once in a lifetime experience for those who had traveled many miles to have an audience with the Pope. People from all over the globe, speechless with solemn anticipation, crammed into clusters on both sides of a central aisle to welcome the Pope's cavalcade. When the procession arrived, they cried out, "*Il Pappa, Il Pappa*" with arms extended, weeping uncontrollably. They truly felt they had been graced with the presence of God. With wide eyes mesmerized by the emotional display, I was captivated.

So, you can imagine (or can you?) Father Greco's total astonishment when he discovered that **my sister had fallen asleep!** She must be deathly ill. There was no other explanation other than we had been up ALL NIGHT. Of course, we couldn't tell him that. The only thing we could think of was a toothache. He wasn't buying it. He made an immediate transatlantic phone call to my mother. "Something's terribly wrong. She was sound asleep during the audience with the Pope!!! You need to take her to the doctor immediately as soon as she gets home!" There was nothing we could say or do.

Soon it was time to say "*Arriverdici Roma*" once again. We exchanged contact information with Piero and Maurizio and assured Father Greco that we would check with the doctor upon arriving in the States. After stuffing our suitcases and sitting on them to close the zippers, we still had a couple dozen items of clothing left over along with our marble bust and our Icelandic pony rug. The only solution was to wear everything! We put on skirt after skirt getting to the point where we had to leave most of them unzipped. We did the same with the sweaters. We each had on about ten skirts and ten sweaters!

We finally arrived in Luxemburg, Icelandic's European hub, and later flew to *Reykjavík* before we were able to head home. We were starving and had time to get something to eat before going to the airport. We could barely walk with all the layers upon layers of clothes, but we managed to hobble to the nearest restaurant. Those crispy **pommes frites** looked so delicious, but we couldn't eat a single thing! Our clothes were so tight. Plus, we looked like we weighed fifty pounds more than usual – without exaggeration. When my mother met us at the airport, SHE DIDN'T RECOGNIZE US AT ALL! She couldn't stop laughing when she saw what we had done. Too much shopping!

It was a whirlwind of a trip – one we would remember all our lives. It had adventure, innocent romance (like the Annette Funicello and Frankie Avalon movies of the sixties), religious pilgrimages, cultural immersion, and lots of fun! We ended up going back – sooner than we expected - thanks to those champagne evenings and The Fund.

Chapter Six

"ALBERT"

Soon after our return from Rome, we had a fire in our house. It was so hot that our refrigerator melted into a little puddle! My mother was at a car repair shop and saw it on the news! She rushed home in a taxi while it was still burning, ran inside, and managed single-handedly to drag out the huge Oriental rug. There was some concern because my high school called and said I was absent that day. Everyone thought I was in the house during the fire, but I had jumped on the bus with my sister that morning when she went back to Clark University in Worcester (where the real rocket scientist, Robert Goddard, taught physics several decades earlier). I neglected to tell my mother. Could she blame me? She was our mentor for spontaneity and adventure! Eventually, everyone discovered that I was safe. The house was not!

My sister graduated from college and took on the responsibility of renovating the house while my mother went to the Hannah Harrison School for Hotel Management in Washington D.C. I went to live with The Doctor at his home in the country.

This wasn't the BIG HOUSE that he built earlier in life in the 1930s when he pursued his love for architecture. We always called it the "big house" to distinguish it from the home he restored in the center of town where I stayed for a bit. Others always referred to it as "The Castle." He called it "the end of the world." It was a 5000 square-foot Tudor-style "stone studded mansion" built by **Italian craftsmen who were The Doctor's former patients**. It served as a way to pay off their medical bills.

The Doctor's house in the center of town

Enclosed by high stone walls, the estate included twenty-six acres of land, $20,000 worth of standing timber, and panoramic views of the Scantic River Valley. There was a subterranean wine cellar, a HUGE IN-GROUND **ROUND** swimming pool sixty feet in diameter, a tennis court, a lily pond, and two trout brooks. We often had picnics there in the summertime. In addition to the main part of the house, there was a four-car garage with full chauffeur's quarters, a billiard room, a tap room, a caretaker's cottage, and a gate lodge. Can you imagine? What a place!

We called it The Big House; others called it The Castle.

The living room was larger than someone's entire house! There was a massive fieldstone "walk-in" fireplace at one end, and at least fifty feet away at the other end were two elegantly curved stairways on each side that met at the top of a second-floor balcony. Huge hand-hewn beams supported the high ceilings, and carved black oak paneling with floral motifs lined the walls. We loved to explore all the secret rooms **hidden** by "floor to ceiling" bookshelves that were really doors. A sunroom, a conservatory, a butler's pantry, and six bedrooms – all with fireplaces and private baths - were also included. The Doctor thought of everything when he designed this work of art. To this day it stands out as the most prestigious property in town.

Across the street, he also designed one of the most unique homes ever constructed. Built on a slant as though a strong gust had literally blown it over, he called it the "Wind Swept Home." The entire structure tilted to the side at a considerable angle – about 45 to 60 degrees. It was a real house with all the normal rooms one would expect but sloping to the right more than the Leaning Tower of Pisa. Eventually, it burned down, and only the fireplace remained. Although architecture was only his hobby, The Doctor gave Frank Lloyd Wright a run for his money!

At one point, The Doctor wanted to move into town, and he decided to sell the Big House. Signs went up and realtors were contacted, but it wasn't moving. **My mother said she could sell it!** She had a Real Estate Broker's License, and she put a **full-page advertisement in the New York Times Sunday Newspaper** even though Manhattan was three hours away. An ad of that size was **very expensive.** (The cost today is $150,000!) Thanks to The Fund, she took a risk and made it happen.

Duke Snider won the World Series and almost bought The Big House.

FOR SALE
Property Worth Quarter Million Dollars!

SELLING PRICE $75,000

Large Photo ... House Proper——Inset .. Gate Lodge

COUNTRY ESTATE, NORMAN ARCHITECTURE, FIELDSTONE CONSTRUCTION, ABOUT 300 ACRES OF LAND.

LOCATION: Quaint New England village (low tax rate); ½-hour flying time and 3-hour driving time from New York City.

ROOF ... Antique, handmade tile.

MAIN FLOOR ... Living room 20x50, vaulted celing with hand-hewn beams (2 stories high). Large fieldstone fireplace occupies one wall. Sitting room, dining room, kitchen, one bedroom, all with fireplace, and latter with complete bath. Sun room, conservatory, butler's pantry and one lavatory.

SECOND FLOOR ... 3 large bedrooms, each with fireplace, complete bath and individual shower.

BASEMENT ... 4-car garage, boiler room, chauffeur's room with fireplace, laundry, billard room, tap room, two lavatories, one with shower. Floors are all tiled.

WINDOWS ... Steel sash casement. All paneling throughout house knotty pine, knotty cedar, quartered oak and mahogany. Heating system—steam, oil, with concealed copper radiation. Hinges, latches and lighting fixtures hand-forged. All baths and lavatories completely tiled (faienced and mosiac), and modern throughout. All rooms are wired for radio and intercommunicating telephone. Floors on first and second floors are planked oak, screwed and pegged.

GROUNDS ... Well landscaped. Lily pond. Subterannean wine and storage cellar. Tennis court, two good trout brooks. Large circular swimming pool (60' in diameter), cemented and natural water supply. Outside living room 14x20, finished in knotty pine with two showers and four dressing rooms. Caretaker's cottage, gate lodge. Roadside bordered by high fieldstone wall. Landing field. Approximately $20,000 worth of standing timber. Within a 4-to-10-mile radius of six outstanding golf courses.

FOR FURTHER INFORMATION .... WRITE **E. KANE** AGENT ... 14 MAPLE STREET, SPRINGFIELD MASSACHUSETTS

Mom sold The Big House twice!

Charlene and Gramma Quaquarelli

Activity developed immediately. My mother always told an amusing story about one interested party. A gentleman called from New York and said he had a client who would like to see "The Castle." He wanted my mother to meet them at the airport because they didn't know anyone in the area. She was happy to do so and waited for them in the terminal. After greeting each other, they started to proceed through Arrivals when DOZENS of young boys and their families dashed up and encircled the client with hopeful expressions, outstretched arms, and autograph books! Perplexed by the reception, my mother said, "I thought you didn't know anyone in this area."

The companion chuckled, "I guess you don't follow baseball. That's Duke Snider, the Silver Fox, and he just won the World Series!"

> On October 4, 1955, the Brooklyn Dodgers won the World Series beating the New York Yankees 2-0. Edwin Donald Snider led Brooklyn to their one and only World Series victory over the Yankees.

My grandfather, an avid baseball fan, just couldn't believe my mother spent the entire afternoon with the "Duke of Flatbush!" He didn't buy the Big House, but my mother sold it – TWICE! I don't think she ever got a commission. Whenever she mentioned it to The Doctor, he just laughed.

Back to the fire in our home – my sister, Nora, went to work on the renovation all by herself. She worked with contractors, made daily trips to home improvement stores, chose color schemes, materials, and appliances. It was beautiful and blue (my mother's favorite color), but Mom said she would have done things differently! We weren't around to help, but my sister had moral support from our next-door neighbor.

When his mother died, Albert came to live with his Uncle Leo, his wife, Rose, and an old Italian grandmother, Gramma Quaquarelli, who used to take care of me when my mother worked at the clinic. On early spring afternoons, I trailed behind Gramma Quaquarelli as she scoured the entire neighborhood for baby dandelions. She had a little pocketknife that she used to uproot the tiny plants. She dropped them into a catch-all "tote bag" that she fashioned out of old clothes. We walked for hours, and when she got home she cleaned them all to get ready for dinner. I think I must have acquired my taste for arugula greens from those dandelions. I love the bitter taste.

When we weren't gathering dandelions, Gramma Quaquarelli sat me down on her tiny twin bed and read to me from the Bible. She gently lifted it from her dresser drawer as though it were a precious piece of porcelain glass. She cautiously turned the well-worn delicate pages and read to me even though it was all in Italian. Then, she turned to somewhat frightening, Medieval-style pictures of Adam and Eve and the dreaded serpent. It was scary, yet her sense of awe was fascinating. I think it helped me cultivate a deep respect for the Bible which returned in my later years.

The two "grandmothers" were a great combination – bitter greens and the Bible from one and Marilyn Monroe and the beach from the other. That was a well-rounded foundation. I had everything I needed in life! It's just like the sentiment in Robert Fulghum's book, *All I Really Need to Know I Learned in Kindergarten*.

Since our home had five acres of land right in the middle of the city, The Doctor built two other homes on the property. Family friends and relatives bought them. There was a rumor that Uncle Leo was supposedly the get-away-driver for "**La Familia**." I don't think so because he often drove us to school - very methodically. We wondered how he ever got away fast if the story were true. Uncle Leo was a very nice man. On the weekends, I always knocked on the door and asked his wife if Leo could come out to play. I guess I thought he was my best friend. Without fail, he put on a light jacket and came out to keep me company. We sat in the big back yard, and he just threw the ball to their dog, Tootsie, who retrieved it again and again. I enjoyed my time there so much that I often refused to go home when Mom called me. Finally, she put my suitcase outside the front door and told me to move over there!

The Doctor's cousin, Ralph, lived in the other house (the one whose sister was a doctor!). His "wife" planted incredible gardens with every variety of flowers known to man. Each week Dorothy provided a huge bouquet of flowers for us to bring to our teachers! Much better than an apple. I guess that's why we were always the teachers' pets.

Albert was a good man – very kind. He was a salesman for a pharmaceutical company. He grieved for his mother who had died, went to church every Sunday, and brought me to all the "father/daughter" communion breakfasts at the Italian church in the South End. He was about my sister's age – maybe a little older – and often checked on her while she lived at home alone. Eventually, he wanted to marry her.

At that point, we all came back home. While reminiscing one evening in the living room, we opened a bottle of champagne (of course). Before we knew it, there was another transatlantic phone call. My sister wasn't sure if she should marry Albert (maybe it was because he gave her a car in place of an engagement ring – too practical, especially when you consider that he put the car payments in her name!). We all thought we should call Father Greco in Rome and get some advice. Father Greco said that such a conversation should take place in person. He didn't have to tell us twice. That very evening we made a withdrawal from The Fund and put everything in motion.

Mom and I planned to go first (on Icelandic, of course). We would drive from Luxemburg to France, visit Sylvie and her family, drive to Switzerland, and cross the Alps into Italy. Nora would meet us in Rome. In the beginning, all went as planned. Things were a little shaky when we picked up the rental car in Luxemburg. My sister had just taught me how to drive. Thankfully, I learned on a car with a standard transmission. That came in handy on the Alps – not so much in Rome. However, I didn't have a license, so Mom had to drive the car out of the rental yard. She hadn't driven a standard for decades, but she managed. Me not having a license didn't seem to matter to us. I'm not sure why.

We always said my mother played the piano by ear but rarely played the game of life by the rules. I think we inherited a bit of that.

We had a great time driving through the French countryside, staying at quaint little inns with balconies and gardens and visiting Sylvie and her family. We fell in love with goose-down duvets in all the hotels and tried to figure out how to bring them home. Everything was fine until one morning in Geneva. We were about to cross the Alps when people in cars going by started yelling out the windows and slapping the sides of their cars. We tried to figure out what we were doing wrong. We kept driving, but they didn't stop. Their cries became more frantic - "*est on feu! est on feu!!*" Our car was on fire – smoke and flames were flying out of the back! Was the engine there? We pulled over to the side and jumped out of the car. Somehow, we got to a repair shop. The owner laughed when we said we needed it right away because we were going to a wedding in Italy that night (there was no wedding). As we later found out, there was no way we were going to drive 200 miles THROUGH THE ALPS in one afternoon.

Mont Blanc was in front of us for hours!

Treacherous roads in the Swiss Alps

We finally got on our way the next morning and drove FOREVER. All we ever saw was Mont Blanc – the highest mountain in the Alps rising about 16,000 feet above sea level. It was constantly in front of us no matter what direction or what distance we drove. We started to wonder how we got there and would we ever get home. My mother screamed every time we approached the hairpin turns and terrifying cliffs up and down each side of every mountain. You come out of one curve in 2nd gear, rev up into 3rd, and then immediately downshift to 2nd to make the next turn – for hours, literally. Cars fly up behind and race around you not even wincing even though others are speeding toward them on the opposite side of the very narrow road. I sure got my practice driving a standard – I felt like Mario Andretti in the Indianapolis 500!

Finally, we crossed the border into Italy and stopped at an **_osteria_** to get a bite to eat. We were famished after driving for so long. It was already nighttime, and the town seemed a little sketchy. The bathroom was even more questionable. My mother managed to pull a cook with a big butcher knife out of the kitchen and stationed him by the door of the "**_bagno_**" so that no one would enter. It worked. We ate something quickly and then continued down a dark, deserted **_autostrada_** toward Rome. To this day, I'm certain that a stork flew over us and almost hit the car!

Soon we arrived at our home away from home – our favorite hotel – The Dinesen. We contacted Piero and Maurizio to take them to dinner. Piero said he would join us later in the week when my sister arrived. Maurizio was available and he joined us with a friend. His hair was now stylishly coiffed, and his chic suit leaned toward high fashion. Europeans always have a certain flair. We managed to have an enjoyable evening in spite of our broken French and lack of Italian. Maurizio said that he and Piero would pick us up at The Dinesen and we would go together to meet my sister at the airport.

In the interim, my mother and I dined and shopped - our favorite pastimes. We ate lunch one day at a local restaurant in a piazza at the bottom of the Spanish Steps. They had a buffet table with a huge assortment of tantalizing appetizers – arancini (deep-fried risotto balls); baked stuffed artichokes; an assortment of bruschetta – some with ricotta and lemon, others with filet mignon topped with roasted red peppers and gorgonzola cheese; and pasta every which way you can imagine - Bolognese, carbonara, pesto. We also enjoyed focaccia, marinated olives, fava beans, and so much more. We asked about the arrangement and understood that we were supposed to go up and help ourselves. We did so – several times. When the bill came, it was an enormous figure. Apparently there was a separate cost for each item, and we sampled them all more than once! Oh, well. We enjoyed every moment.

Piero and Maurizio arrived promptly on the big day, and we all headed to ***Leonardo Da Vinci Aeroporto***. While we were waiting in Arrivals, we decided to look at the passenger list to confirm that my sister was on the plane. We ran our fingers down the alphabetical list and there she was. Perfect! We only scanned down to the K's. We should have kept going to the M's!

We waited with excitement until the passengers disembarked. We were thrilled when we saw her - all four of us beaming with anticipation. Then, suddenly, my mother and I froze like deer caught in headlights. My sister stepped out of the plane and, lo and behold, **Albert was right behind her!** We tried to hide our shock and bewilderment, but our faces gave us away. I started saying, "***mon oncle, mon oncle***," (my uncle) but they weren't buying it. Piero's countenance fell or should I say collapsed. His face lost its color and his eyes welled up with tears. I guess my sister didn't know we were planning to pick her up with Piero and Maurizio. There were no cell phones back then for last minute modifications.

Awkward introductions were made, and somehow, **we convinced Albert to take a taxi with my mother** back to the train station and then to the hotel. My sister and I rode with Piero and Maurizio! Had to. It was a tiny car. Mom felt badly for Albert. He was crying uncontrollably until he saw a former business client to whom he sold pharmaceutical supplies. Apparently, he quickly changed modes and went into his sales pitch. My mother's compassion started to fade.

When they arrived at the train station, my mother said they should walk to the hotel hoping to give us some extra time with Piero and Maurizio. While we had tea in the hotel's beautiful dining room, my mother walked and walked and tried to console Albert. His tale of woe must have been tiresome because she said they should stop and have an ***aperitivo*** at one of the outdoor cafes on the way. In the middle of it all, she met a handsome admirer, and they made plans to meet again. Finally, they arrived at The Dinesen after walking halfway across Rome.

That's when the entire event became a classic farce or **commedia dell'arte**. Mom was exhausted and Albert was frantic. We pushed Piero and Maurizio out the infamous side door just in time (reminiscent of our earlier adventures with Piero, Maurizio and Father Greco). Albert was pacing up and down shouting, "I need to see Father Greco and make my confession!" (not that he did anything bad - Catholics just like to confess a lot)

He ran up to his room, opened the windows and started swinging love notes back and forth to the window below. Mom stuck her head out and shouted up to Albert that this was her room, not my sister's. The guests in the courtyard below were amused. It was just another day in the city of love. We were running back and forth trying to figure out what to do. We put Albert in a taxi and ushered him off to the rectory to see Father Greco. He made his confession while we went out to dinner. I admit it sounds insensitive. We just figured Albert was in good hands. He was where he wanted to be, and so were we.

When Albert came back, he had decided that he should fly back home to the States the next day! He had just spent $700 on a last-minute flight to accompany my sister. They didn't take the more economical Icelandic route. Now he was going back after one day. He didn't even see Rome (AND HE WAS ITALIAN!). I guess Father Greco wanted to talk to us by ourselves. Albert left the following morning, and we all went out to dinner at **Scoglio's** around the corner from the monastery where we were serenaded with our favorite Italian songs – "Summertime in Venice," "Fascination," and our favorite – "**Al Di La**."

Soon it was time for us to say **"*Arrivederci Roma*"** once again. The only problem was that the rental car could not be returned in Italy. There was another issue. It wouldn't start on its own. We always had to park on a hill so that we could roll down and kick start it. So, you may be able to imagine my mother's concern when we decided to go back first (school for me) and leave her all alone to return the car in France. To this day, I don't know how she drove in Rome. NYC can't even begin to compare with driving in the eternal city.

After we left, my mother had an interesting experience while dining in The Dinesen one evening. Remember, this very tranquil and quaint boutique hotel was only one block from the Via Veneto and all the foreign embassies. Lots of VIPs preferred to lodge there to circumvent the glamorous paparazzi-laden boulevard. Just as soon as she was seated, a gentleman approached and asked if she would be willing to dine at the table of a very dignified aristocrat sitting at the far end of the dining room so that he could practice English. She was happy to do so, and they spent a very enjoyable evening together. When he heard about her plight with the rental car, he volunteered to have a driver take it to France and he would provide a plane to take her wherever she wanted to go. She declined. They took an evening stroll after dinner, and my mother noticed that a "detachment" of men - all with an imposing physical stature - trailed at a short distance everywhere they went. She kept turning around inconspicuously to determine who they were and what they were doing. When she returned to The Dinesen, her curiosity got the best of her, and she asked the concierge about them. To her surprise, she discovered **she had just dined with the Shah of Iran.**

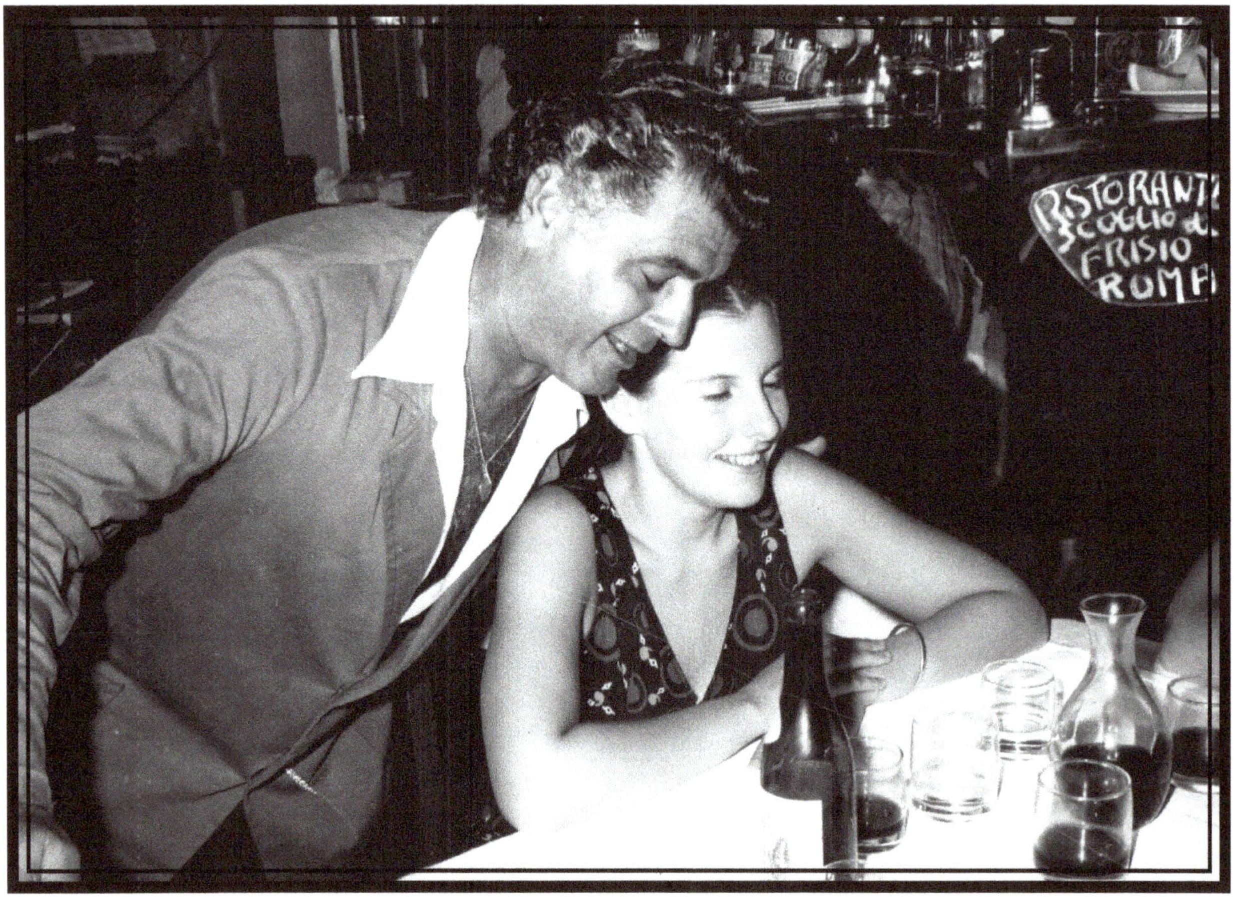
RISTORANT
SCOGLIO
FRISIO
ROM

Serenaded at dinner at Ristorante Lo Scoglio di Friso in Rome

Mohammad Reza Pavi
Mom ate dinner with the Shah of Iran!

Although my mother refused the Shah's very generous invitation, she did meet the "handsome admirer" from the outdoor café where she and Albert had stopped for some refreshment during their "walk-a-bout" on the way in from the airport. He took her to dinner, and she suggested **Scoglio's** (the restaurant down the road from the monastery) because of its convivial atmosphere with the serenading musicians. Just as the violinists approached her table, SHE GLANCED UP AND SAW FATHER GRECO AND NORMA'S BROTHER, WALTER, DINING ACROSS THE ROOM! She just smiled graciously and waved - didn't even try to explain how she ended up eating dinner with a complete stranger halfway around the world from home. At least they didn't find out that she almost flew off with the Shah of Iran.

Somehow my mother managed to drive up to the French border to return the rental car. As usual, the journey was not without excitement. She actually picked up a hitchhiker on the way. Don't ask me why. It was somewhat uncharacteristic of her even though hitchhiking was much more common back in the sixties. (A couple of years later I hitchhiked around Europe **all alone**. I thought I had to "find myself.") However, my mother must have had second thoughts on the drive. Every time the hitchhiker moved and startled her, she jumped and caused the car to continually swerve into oncoming traffic. Although she was afraid, he must have been terrified. He banged on the door repeatedly and insisted that she stop the car immediately and let him out!

When she finally arrived in Nice, France, just fifteen miles after crossing the Italian border, it was very late at night. Her hotel room was gone! She was exhausted and desperate. "What could she do? Where could she stay?" she pleaded. Finally, to alleviate her anguish, they provided a room that was normally reserved for employees. Hoping to finally unwind after driving 300 miles, she opened the last bottle of ASTI SPUMANTE WHICH WE PURCHASED IN BULK IN ITALY. After all, she couldn't just throw it out before boarding the plane the next day. I guess it must have bounced around on the trip, because when she uncorked the bottle, there was a **VERY LOUD POP. Everyone came running and pounded on the door. They thought she shot herself!**

The following day she returned the car, flew to Majorca where she pampered herself with a luxurious spa treatment, and then to Portugal where all her meals were served with a fried egg on top! Maybe it was James Michener's *Iberia* or *The Drifters* - one of them triggered her desire to go to such places. Years later, because of those books, we visited Portugal's ***Algarve*** on the Mediterranean Coast and discovered Europe's best kept secret.

Albert eventually married and had a family and children. That arrangement was more suitable for him. Like my mother, my sister is a free spirit. She was probably too eccentric and adventurous for Albert. We ran into him years later. He was happy.

The Furcolo Clinic

Chapter Seven

"BATS IN THE BELFRY: THE CLINIC"

The Furcolo Clinic was the center of our universe for many years. It was a thriving enterprise comprised of three floors of doctors' offices on each side of huge waiting rooms. It was a beautiful stone mansion with round rooms and towers and was located on the edge of downtown and across the street from the Quadrangle which housed the city's central library and museums. It even had tunnels that ran under the street to offices on the other side. Originally, it was the site of the Monarch Life Insurance Company. There was a glimpse of it in the movie, *The Reincarnation of Peter Proud*.

The Doctor bought the building and moved his practice there after a car crushed his leg and made it impossible for him to conduct long hours of surgery. My mother accompanied him to the clinic as his nurse and office manager.

From the time we were little, we would go to the clinic after school. Mom and The Doctor gave us little jobs to do. Most of the time we counted pills for prescriptions and put them into envelopes that would be dispensed to patients. The medical world was commonplace to us and that may be why they groomed my sister to be a doctor. They didn't have such hopes for me after I fainted when I saw The Doctor remove a cast from a woman's broken arm. The flesh was so white and emaciated. I fell right to the floor and fainted. They had to revive me with smelling salts.

After my mother returned from the hotel management school in Washington D.C., she seemed resolved to change directions in life. She was actually offered a position to "open" a Marriott in Chicago. She had impressed her instructors at the school with a detailed list of corrections that needed to be made on a new hotel that was "ready to go" or so they thought. She turned down the offer and came back home. Another sacrifice – she didn't want to uproot her girls.

The original plan was to have Albert buy our house and settle there with my sister when they were married. After the trip to Rome, we had to move on to Plan B. The wedding was off, and my mother sent our gowns to Father Greco to be redesigned into vestments for the clergy. She was upset that a family friend helped my sister pick out her wedding dress while she was in D.C. It was a tradition usually reserved for the mother of the bride. Since that didn't happen, she packed up the dresses and sent them off to Rome.

My mother often discarded items that disturbed her. When we didn't clean our bedrooms after repeated requests, she opened the windows on the second floor of our house and threw out all of our clothes. Most were strewn across the front yard and on top of the lilac bushes. I'm not sure what our neighbors thought. Another time, when we didn't wash the dishes – again after many "requests" – she dragged in a 30-gallon rubbish barrel and dumped in all the dirty dishes!

During this period, The Doctor's health was starting to fail. Berkshire Downs and Rahar's Inn had gotten the best of him. He basically closed his practice but drove into town each day to sit in his office and visit with old patients and friends. Then, at noon, we went to lunch at some of our old favorite places. The Doctor would have a martini, and my sister and I would linger there with him for a leisurely lunch which usually lasted most of the afternoon.

We were all in some sort of transition in our lives, so we decided to go on a cruise (probably due to a little champagne in the living room one evening and The Fund.) We went with The Doctor, his housekeeper (Hazel), and the three of us. The Doctor had his own cabin, and somehow the four women shared another one. My sister and I had the top bunks. It was an Italian line, and we LOVED the meals and the Italian crew. They waited on us hand and foot, and we became hooked on cruising.

We should have known that things were not quite right when we all met in New York, and Hazel arrived with a big box of donuts for the next morning. We looked at each other puzzled and suddenly realized that she had no concept of where we were going and that we did not have to worry about food for breakfast on a cruise ship. Her dementia (?) became more apparent when she regularly approached the maître d' in the dining room and asked him to call a taxi for her to go home! The officers were quite concerned and told us she often wandered into the crew's quarters at night.

One evening, after we put the adults to bed, my sister and I had two double dates **simultaneously** at opposite ends of the ship. We met two very nice young men and we agreed to meet them that evening in the lounge located in the "forward" area of the ship. We met two others and arranged a date **at the same time** in the "aft" area of the ship. At half-hour intervals, we would excuse ourselves to use the ladies' room and go meet our second dates at the other end of the vessel. We were so silly, laughing hysterically at what we pulled off each time we hurried to return to our other engagement. We went back and forth a few times. It was so much fun until we looked up and saw Hazel in a long, flowing *négligée* up in the lounge trying to demand a taxi once again. I think we felt obligated to go up and rescue her and bring her back to our cabin. That was the end of our "double, double dates!"

Eventually, The Doctor didn't drive into the clinic as often and we were worried about his health and whether he was eating regular meals. It seemed like Hazel forgot to cook most of the time. We checked on them regularly and stocked the cupboards with SlimFast hoping to get some sort of nourishment into them. That's when the Doctor decided to sell The Clinic. He wasn't in the right frame of mind to wheel and deal like in his early days. When he decided to sell way below value, my mother said, "I'll buy it!" She put things in motion by selling our home and obtained a mortgage that would be held by The Doctor's son, the former Governor of Massachusetts.

Suddenly, Mom announced that our home had been sold, and she and Nora ended up with the burden of moving twenty years of accumulated possessions out of our very large house. I was away at college. Somehow they managed and moved lock, stock, and barrel to The Clinic - filling up most of the three floors. The huge central waiting rooms became our living rooms. (Visitors were stunned when the elevator doors opened, and they were right in the middle of our home.) The laboratories became the kitchens. We had lots of bathrooms, and the former doctors' offices became our bedrooms. We seemed to change floors often and finally settled in on the second floor.

It might seem like my mother had **Bats in the Belfry** to move to such a place. We didn't think so, but she did have bats! They swarmed all around downtown every night. We think they came from the old Milton Bradly factory nearby, and they often ended up inside The Clinic. One time, Mom had just taken a bath when one started zigzagging back and forth in that confined space aiming directly at her or so she thought. She couldn't run out because she was in the tub! She acted fast and grabbed the hairspray while screaming at the top of her lungs. I don't know who was more afraid – Mom or the bat!

All of the doctors were gone, but soon, some very interesting tenants moved in. My mother needed the rental income to pay what must have been a very large mortgage. We had Mr. Newlands in one corner of the second floor. He was a very pleasant and polite gentleman. We only saw him coming and going always wearing a business suit and a felt-brimmed fedora. A tall stack of neatly folded Wall Street Journals was placed outside his doorway each week. We imagined he was very involved in the stock market. We never found out.

Stanley Rogers lived in one corner of the third floor. He was an eccentric artist who actually had two of his large, **very abstract** paintings in the George Walter Vincent Smith Art Museum in the Quadrangle. Most nights, Stanley would go out to the parking lot behind The Clinic and charge people for parking when they went to the Arcade Movie Theater next door (where my grandmother brought us to all the Marilyn Monroe movies when we were children). Stanley stayed out just long enough to be able to buy a fifth of vodka. Then, he would go up to his room, **BLAST** Tchaikovsky's *1812 Overture*, and paint. The musical selection, which commemorated Russia's defense against Napoleon's invasion, was known for its "climatic volley of cannon fire, ringing chimes, and a brass fanfare finale." We always knew when Stanley was hard at work creating his masterpieces.

Mr. Holland lived across from Stanley. He had very large professional drafting tables in his room and was continually working on blueprints. He said he designed the rotor system for helicopter propellers which enabled them to take off vertically and to hover in one place. We think it might have been possible because his résumé included multiple engineering degrees from Rutgers University, and he formerly owned and managed several companies in New York which specialized in the construction of "Special Machinery." At one point, he told Mom that he came from another planet. I'm not sure if she thought he was kidding or not. He was a mysterious

Chanya

gentleman. Eventually, he lost his leg from diabetes and my mother cared for him between hospital visits. She knew how to clean and dress the wound. He died on Mother's Day in the hospital. I remember because we insisted on taking my mother out to dinner to celebrate. She hesitated because she knew he was very ill at that time. He died alone while we were at dinner. My mother never forgave herself (or us?).

We also had an exchange student from Guatemala named Jonas, another man who changed his last name to Eros, and a group of real-life nomadic gypsies who refused to leave or pay their rent. When all else failed, my mother called an old friend. He might have been a sheriff. We don't know what he said or did, but they were gone the next morning. No trace of them remained.

My mother also brought home lots of dogs who were about to be euthanized at the local shelter down the road which we visited frequently. We had a huge Great Dane named Tericka, a little blind mutt of a dog appropriately named Muttsie, and a tiny black dog named Bootsie and alternately called Sweet Pea because he had to be put out on the fire escape to go to the bathroom. Scallywag had beautiful long hair and often went sailing with my mother on a friend's sailboat. Minutiae, who must have been small and trivial in his owner's mind, was another addition. I think there were others who came and went. We didn't have them all at once. My mother just couldn't bear to see them put to sleep. She eventually found homes for all of them but kept a tiny white American Eskimo. She named her Chanya after a Russian folk song that she liked called "**Ochi Chyernye**" (Dark Eyes).

During this period, my mother went to work at a local inn. Celebrities sometimes stayed there when they had concerts in town. James Brown gave her an autographed self-portrait and dedicated it to "Eileen, a Real Soul Sister." She also met the two famous American pianists, Ferrante & Teicher. Mom enjoyed working at the inn especially because of the camaraderie among the staff members. They all became good friends. One gentleman from Great Britain was an excellent ballroom dancer. We often invited him to our leisurely two-hour dinners, and he taught us how to dance. My mother didn't need lessons. She had always been an excellent ballroom dancer. She had so much grace and seemed to glide across the floor with no effort whatsoever. I don't know how or where she ever learned. She spent most of her childhood with nuns - so much so that they just expected she would join the convent when she grew up. She had different plans.

My sister and I were pretty good at the Cha-Cha – thanks to the invasion of Brazil's Bossa Nova during the sixties – but our British friend taught us how to dance the Foxtrot, Samba, Tango, and Waltz. It was so much fun, and we became fairly good dancers. It actually caused me to try to stow away on a cruise ship one time. I just wanted to keep dancing. My mother didn't even try to stop me! They recognized me from the previous week and caught me just as they were about to sail. They quickly and quietly escorted me out by way of the kitchen gangplank. My family was long gone, so I had to take a bus back to Massachusetts.

This may be hard to believe, but I had more fun at home dining and dancing than on my college campus. I rearranged my class schedule at school so that I could hop on the bus outside the student union on Thursdays and return to school on Mondays. We could dine and dance all weekend!

While at work, my mother and our British friend filled the monotony with intrigue and adventure. She read the New York Times and always scanned the classifieds looking for interesting prospects. One time she found an apartment for rent right at the bottom of the Via Veneto, Rome's most exclusive boulevard always filled with movie stars, embassies, and plenty of paparazzi. She wrote immediately, and we were almost at the point of another transatlantic phone call and flight until she realized that she mixed up the zeros converting **Lire** to dollars. She thought the rent was $100 per month (1970s), but it was actually $1000 per month (equivalent to about $8000 per month today)! Way too expensive!

Soon after, an advertisement for the sale of a castle in Orvieto, Italy, was too enticing to resist. She wrote to the agents involved and **sort of implied** that she represented our British friend who was very much interested in purchasing the estate. In a roundabout way, **she may have suggested that he owned the inn where they worked**. There was a lot of correspondence, a little champagne one evening, a sizable withdrawal from The Fund, and suddenly we were on our way to assess the property for "interested parties!"

This castle was the real deal! ***Castello del Poggio***, originally built as a fortress, stood high on a mountain with a 360-degree panoramic view of all of Umbria. It dated back to the 11th century and had even been the home of Lucrezia Borgia (1480-1590), the daughter of Pope Alexander VI who was infamous for her skillful use of poison-filled rings to eliminate political rivals. When we went to Orvieto, the castle was owned by the widow of the famous Italian American vaudeville comedian, Jimmy Savo. She introduced herself as Madame Savo.

We flew into Rome, rented a car, and soon arrived on the outskirts of Orvieto. Madame Savo reserved some rooms for us in a "modern" American style motel – flat, one story, plain - no ambience whatsoever. She assumed we'd prefer such a place rather than the charming, tastefully decorated, old-world boutique hotels. We didn't even check in. Instead, we drove about a thousand feet up to the very picturesque, medieval hill town and found more suitable accommodations for the first night.

Orvieto (about an hour's drive north of Rome) has been described as Italy's hidden gem. The town is built on top of underground caves and tunnels and boasts some of the best white wine and the most beautiful hand-painted pottery in the world. It has a central piazza with a huge cathedral which houses floor to ceiling frescos painted by the famous artist, Luca Signorelli.

Early the next morning, my mother set out early to explore and "found" Hotel Posta – our home away from home for the next two weeks. She was meandering along the very narrow streets when a huge truck came barreling down the road. Since there were no sidewalks, she had no choice but to back up very quickly into the nearest open door. She found herself in the lobby of a very quaint ***albergo*** where she was welcomed by a somewhat plump child with a beaming smile – "***Maximo***" – or Max, the son of the ***Proprietaria***. Needless to say, we relocated immediately.

Orvieto, Italy

The narrow streets in Orvieto

Handmade ceramics from Orvieto

We carried home dinner service for eight.

A small family-owned *ristorante* directly across the "street" just beckoned us as soon as the dinner hour arrived. The husband greeted us with an out-stretched hand indicating that we should sit at the best table. His wife also welcomed us from the kitchen with a full apron, rosy cheeks, and a glint in her eyes. The two sons, Frankie (must have been *Francesco)* and *Giancarlo*, graciously presented menus and homemade wine from the caves directly below the restaurant. We dined there **every** night for two weeks!

The next day, we planned to begin our "appraisal" of the castle. Madame Savo **insisted that we arrive in the evening** which seemed very odd to us. So, at twilight, we drove down the mountain from the town of Orvieto and followed very vague directions to the bottom of another peak with *Castello del Poggio* looming over the entire valley. Madame Savo assured us her gardener would meet us and take us up to the castle.

When we arrived, an elderly workhand with a wizened face full of folds and wrinkles greeted us from a rickety old cart pulled by a donkey. His arthritic hands, knotted up from years of manual labor, motioned to follow him up the side of the mountain on a **rocky path no wider than our tiny European car** – not to mention the fact that it was dark! Once again, we wondered what kind of fiasco we had gotten ourselves into, or should I say, what my mother and The Fund had gotten us into. Our car basically crawled up the side of the cliffs VERY SLOWLY! We had no choice. The donkey took his time scaling the arduous path up and up and up. We contemplated turning around, but that wasn't even possible on such a narrow trail. The standard transmission didn't make it any easier. After about twenty minutes at five miles an hour and on the brink of a nervous breakdown, we arrived at the top.

An incredible sight awaited. **Every tower, every arch, and every window had enormous torches on fire rippling in the wind!** There seemed to be hundreds of them! Now we knew why she wanted us to arrive at night. Then we were struck by the most dramatic sight of all – Madame Savo suddenly appeared at the very top of the highest balcony **laughing hysterically.** Dressed in a full-length white gown with layers of silk whipping around in the gusts of wind that were so strong at such a height, she waved her arms back and forth frantically. It was scary – alarming! We didn't know what to do – how to escape.

Our strange guide hobbled up the path and summoned us to follow him to the foreboding entrance of the gatehouse. I don't know who spoke first, but we were all on the same wavelength. In frantic, half whispers, Nora and I tried to stop our mother. "Don't go in! We can't go in. Act like you need a drink of water. Sit on that rock. Pretend you're going to faint!"

Finally, Madame Savo came down to ground level utterly thrilled with excitement. Resembling Carol Channing in the musical, *Hello Dolly*, with big, beaming eyes and a wide Cheshire Cat grin, she exclaimed, "**I wanted you to have the full experience - to see the castle in all of its splendor as it appeared at the height of the Medieval ages.**"

We were speechless. We decided it was safe to enter but couldn't see anything to speak of because there was no electricity! I don't think she gave us a glass of wine or anything. The gardener brought my mother some water, but we were afraid to drink it. We could have used something a little stronger at that point. To this day, I don't know how we got back to the hotel. I think there was more of a main road that we took on the following days when we did our "assessment for interested buyers" back home.

Day after day for two weeks, we drove to the castle, took measurements, made lists of contents, and photographed everything. The going form of photography at the time was slide film. Photos were either shown from a slide projector or later developed into prints. We took a ton of them. Unfortunately, a few years later, some kids blew up the trunk of my car, and most of the slides melted! We had a few remnants left.

The castle actually had some priceless antiquities. There were huge, wall-size paintings in elaborate gold gilt frames which were a work of art in themselves. An authentic Louis the Fourteenth billiards table (according to Madame Savo) filled an entire room. We started to do a real appraisal because it seemed like we had stumbled upon some very valuable pieces.

We told Madame Savo we would draw up a contract (my sister typed it in an office supply store). Arrangements were made to see a lawyer in Venice, and we had a farewell party at our favorite little restaurant across from our hotel. We invited Madame Savo, *Il Colonnello,* her gentleman friend, and a friendly architect who had some sort of title like *Il Geometrico* (we just called him the geometric). Another guest was someone official – maybe the mayor of the town? There were about ten of us all together. Our friends in the restaurant were thrilled that we brought such a distinguished group to their humble establishment. It was so festive. Several courses of delicious Umbrian specialties were presented one after the other, and carafes of Orvieto wine from the cellars below were flowing. The Fund made it all possible.

It was not an imposition to make the long trip to see a lawyer in Venice because the "Floating City" is spectacular! It's our favorite place in the world and also the most unique. "Built" on more than 100 tiny islands separated by 200+ canals and connected by about 400 decorative bridges, the ONLY MODE OF TRANSPORTATION IS BY WATER. People are familiar with gondolas, but did you know that taxis, buses, limousines, ambulances, fire vehicles – you name it – they are all boats! It takes a few days, but suddenly you realize that you haven't heard any traffic whatsoever. The colors, the architecture - pure elegance and enchantment.

When we met with the lawyer, we learned that Italy would not let priceless antiquities leave the country. In the final analysis, everything belonged to them. We informed Madame Savo that our British friend "whom we represented in the sale" regrettably declined. A couple of years later, on another trip to Rome, my mother and I drove up to Orvieto to see our friends in the restaurant. It was a Sunday, and they were closed for the day. I suppose the parents are long gone now. We never saw them again. Very pleasant memories remain to this day.

Soon after we returned to the States, the Redevelopment Authority in our city informed my mother that they would be taking The Clinic by eminent domain! She tried to fight them, even hired prominent Jewish lawyers. She presented plans to build an exclusive hotel on the premises. Nothing worked. Like they say, you can't fight city hall. It was still difficult for women to be respected in business circles in those days. Later we realized that some type of payoff might have been the solution. Too little, too late.

Historic Commissions didn't exist at the time to protect a significant example of notable architecture like The Furcolo Clinic. The Redevelopment Authority took it and "paved paradise to put up a literal parking lot" as Joni Mitchell so aptly expressed. What a shame. My mother salvaged the carved etching on the front of the building when bulldozers reduced it to rubble. Funds were provided to "relocate" my mother and sister. They each bought a home. I said I was living on campus and didn't need to be relocated – probably one of the most foolish things I have done in my life.

My mother had the option of relocating to a magnificent mansion with an additional house on the land. By that point in life, she must have had her fill of property, upkeep, and financial responsibility. Our home, the beach house at Giant's Neck, Rahar's Inn, her mother's house, a townhouse rental on historic Mattoon Street, and finally, The Furcolo Clinic – that was a lot for one woman in one lifetime. Deadlines were approaching for relocation, so she chose a small ranch house with a little garden. It didn't suit her. Thankfully, it was temporary, and The Fund kept her going until the next adventure.

Castello del Poggio

Mom by the castle gate

Louis the Fourteenth billiard table in Castello del Poggio

A celebration dinner in Orvieto with Madame Savo and friends

Venice: The Floating City

Enchantment in Venice

Chapter 8

"HOW PEOPLE GRIEVE"

I've been to all types of funerals. Some are very solemn; it's a crime to even smile. At others, loved ones fall over and faint out of despair. They howl in grief and try to crawl into the casket because they can't bear to let their loved ones go. A good Irish funeral is a celebration of life, and the Jameson (Irish Whiskey) is flowing freely. My mother said that her grandfather was a professional mourner in Ireland. He was hired to wail songs of mourning all night. So, I understood that people grieve in different ways, but I witnessed a new phenomenon at The Doctor's funeral.

Shortly after he sold the clinic, The Doctor died at the age of 83 (1888 – 1971). One disturbing memory of his funeral remains to this day. We were in the Italian church in the South End, and hundreds were there. The coffin prominently graced the altar. The Doctor's son (the former Governor of Massachusetts) and his sons and their wives were all in the front. The Doctor's wife and second son had relocated to California decades earlier. Apparently, they never divorced – wasn't done in those days, especially in the Catholic Church. They were not present. We were directed to the far side - ten or fifteen rows back - the area reserved for **acquaintances**.

When the Mass finished, the pallbearers approached the casket. As the procession passed, the grandsons' wives began to sob! They covered their faces with their hands and their chests heaved up and down. I was bewildered by their reaction.

Mom and The Doctor
The end of an era

We watched, and I wondered – who were these people? They never knew The Doctor. We had spent our entire lives with him – every day and night, every vacation, every holiday, every special occasion. The only time I ever remember hearing anything about The Doctor and his son being together was during the political campaign for Governor. Did he even meet the wives of the grandsons? Was there ever a phone call on a holiday? Maybe. Not that I knew of. Why were they crying uncontrollably? **I felt like they robbed something from us that didn't belong to them – the right to grieve for a loved one.**

The Furcolo family gravesite in New Haven, Connecticut

My mother stood on the sidelines with quiet dignity. Years earlier, she told me how impressed she was by Jackie Kennedy and the way she manifested such poise and dignified decorum at the gravesite during the funeral of her husband, President Kennedy. That was a quality my mother had mastered. I never asked her how she really felt that day.

We joined the cavalcade that carried The Doctor to New Haven where he had been raised, attended Yale University and the Yale School of Medicine, and was now being buried. My sister said that his son gave us each a flower to put on the grave before the casket was lowered into the ground. For years, my mother tried to get back to New Haven because The Doctor made her promise that she would visit the grave of his mother. We finally made it and planted three roses there - one for each of us. The Doctor always told Mom that she could be buried there as well. She preferred the Old Cemetery in the country town where The Doctor lived most of his life. She used The Fund to buy plots for all of us. Little did we know that another adventure awaited in that Old Cemetery many years later.

When we returned from the funeral, a small group went to The Esquire Lounge where we often ate lunch with The Doctor and where they always kept a bottle of Dry Sack just for him. We each had a drink of sherry in The Doctor's honor and finished the bottle.

It was sad. An era had passed, and we were all beginning a new chapter in our lives. Yes, people grieve in different ways. **We went on cruises.**

Cruising became our favorite way to travel. We loved the "traditional cruise lines" where guests dressed for dinner and enjoyed cocktails and piano music in the lounges beforehand. Nightly, the same servers waited at attention and accommodated every whim. If we couldn't decide between lobster or rack of lamb – no problem. They just brought both. We seriously considered bringing the waiters home with us.

We became regulars (Mariners) on Holland America and sailed on most of their ships repeatedly. The officers were Dutch, and the crew members were from Indonesia and the Philippines. The Dutch officers were very formal; the crew members were extremely warm and congenial. For a while, we cruised two or three times a year and always preferred to embark in Boston or New York. We didn't have to worry about flights and other travel arrangements. We just drove to the port, dropped off our car with the valet, and headed to the Lido for a scrumptious lunch.

Most of the time we traveled in a party of six. Mom withdrew from The Fund and paid FOR EVERYTHING. When all was said and done, a week cost several thousand dollars! She wasn't wealthy – far from it. During those years, she often worked two jobs to make ends meet, but she always saved to build up The Fund. When I think about spending that much money on ONE WEEK, I shudder. However, that was always my mother's philosophy – the time spent together was as important as sustenance. Beauty, wonder, pleasure – they're just as vital as the necessities in life. They WERE the necessities in her mind – the real "matters of consequence" (from *The Little Prince*).

> If thou of fortune be bereft,
> and in thy store there be but left
> two loaves, sell one, and with the
> dole, buy hyacinths to feed thy soul
>
> John Greenleaf Whittier

Cruising so often enabled us to learn all the tricks of the trade. We discovered that you don't have to limit yourselves to the complimentary watered-down screwdrivers and white wine carried high on trays at the Captain's Welcome Party. No one realizes, but all you have to do is request a specialty cocktail, and they'll go to an adjacent lounge and bring back a Belvedere martini or a ***piña colada*** – no charge. We always had one at the party and another to bring down to dinner.

Here's more "insider information." Before cruising, request an officer to sit at your dinner table on the formal nights. You learn a lot about ship life behind the scenes. More importantly, the wine served at dinner is on the house! When they ask if you would like red or white, just say, "Both!" Dry cleaning is expensive, but they will press everything you have laundered for a minimal fee – even lingerie! If you want to bring your own wine on board – maybe a favorite or a special vintage – ask for it to be uncorked in your cabin to avoid the corkage fee in the dining room.

My mother cruised so much that she received all kinds of medals and special perks. There were only one or two guests in her category on each cruise. I believe she cruised 500,000 miles!

The only other guest who surpassed her had cruised 700,000 miles. As a result, they were invited to a VIP luncheon or cocktail party with the Captain and other officers. It was very exclusive. Of course, she insisted that we accompany her. She wore the same special evening dress to meet the captain of each ship. It was an elegant, dark navy-blue crepe with a white satin shawl collar. After so many cruises, it eventually wore out, so I made her an identical one! She was so happy. We were back in action!

Twice we were invited to the inauguration of a new ship the night before it sailed for the first time. It was a very special event for travel agents, guests who had sailed an enormous number of miles, and other bigwigs. We drove to Boston, checked into a Marriott, and took a taxi to the port. They took us on tours of the ship (which we skipped out of immediately to sample martinis in the lounges), "wined and dined us" the entire evening, presented samples of all the shows, and served after-dinner cordials and refreshments in the lounges – all complimentary. It was really extravagant.

Soon, one-week cruises were not sufficient. It always takes one or two days to relax and acclimate to cruise life. You enjoy days 3 and 4 and then all you can think about is returning to reality. We graduated to a ten-day itinerary and then to two weeks. Much better! We also discovered that world-class entertainment is presented on the longer cruises since they are often segments of world cruises. The shipping lines really cater to passengers who sail with them for months at a time (my goal in life). They also have dance hosts to entertain the single, older (often very wealthy) women like in the movie *Out to Sea* with Jack Lemmon and Walter Matthau. I didn't fit that description, but I always tried to cut in front of them to make myself available to dance.

The key to long cruising is to walk the decks AFTER EACH MEAL. Don't eat again unless you walk a mile. One time I walked with a woman who was on a three-month cruise! She said it was like moving into a condo for a little while. Another gentleman LIVED on the cruise ship! For real. Figure it's a lot cheaper than a retirement community that usually runs about $3000 a month. (How do I know? My mother lived in one in her later years. Thankfully, The Fund came through again but more about that later.) Living on a ship, you have a doctor and a dentist on board, nightly entertainment, and exciting ports. Not to mention all the food!

It's definitely something to consider if you have a measure of health and no family or maybe if you do have family! Just kidding!

As usual, we had some exciting moments on the cruises. One time, my sister, Nora, decided to jump ship and stay in Nassau with - guess who – our British friend from our dancing days. (Remember the "investor" whom we represented at the castle in Orvieto?) The three of us had been on scooters touring the island (bad idea - they drive on the left). We almost missed the ship. The tugboat was already in place ready to pull the behemoth out to sea. All the gangplanks had been lifted! I had to jump across the water down by the galley where they loaded supplies. Several crew members extended their arms and yelled, "Jump! Jump!" It was really a spectacle. The passengers on the upper decks were cheering when I successfully made the leap. In the meantime, my mother was up on the Lido Deck trying to throw big display cheeses down to my sister so that they would have some food. It was quite exciting. My sister and our British friend eventually flew home. The officers were not happy – lots of paperwork and red tape when someone jumps ship!

Another time a group of elderly senior citizens were disembarking to tour the island, and one woman tripped and fell down. My husband ran to her rescue, got her some water, and stayed with her until some crew members came to help. They asked his name, and from that point on, everywhere we went on board, they would all call out to him, "Dino! Dino!" Of course, they all voted for him in the talent show when he sang his favorite Frank Sinatra tunes – "The Way You Look Tonight," "Fly Me to the Moon," and "Night and Day." He became so well known on board that he was always asked to be Mr. Rotterdam, Mr. Noordam, Mr. Statendam – all the "Dam" ships.

We thought we had done it all especially when we cruised the Mediterranean, visited exotic places like Casablanca and Tunisia where we shopped in the souks, and took the trams up to see the Barbary Apes in Gibraltar. Then we discovered the jazz cruises!

Some of the best musicians IN THE WORLD spent the entire week on the cruise, provided the afternoon and evening entertainment, and jammed with each other into the wee hours of the night. During the "off hours" they just relaxed with the rest of the passengers. Just imagine – on one cruise, we saw Dave Brubeck and Paul Desmond along with the band playing "Take

Mom cruised about 500,000 miles with Holland America.

Five" and "Blue Rondo a La Turk," Stan Getz of "The Girl from Ipanema" fame, The Duke Ellington Orchestra conducted by his son, Mercer Ellington, and playing some of my mother's favorites, "Satin Doll" and "The A Train," Sarah Vaughan, Dizzy Gillespie, Earl "Fatha" Hines on the piano, Carmen McRae, Joe Williams, and more – ALL IN ONE WEEK! We must have gone on at least ten jazz cruises, and each lineup was just as fantastic. Our one regret – missing the one with Ray Charles.

Our love for cruising never diminished. However, we took a short interlude because my mother decided to get married at the age of 75 after being a widow for forty years! Did we open a bottle of champagne one evening like in the past? No, I don't think so. She made this choice on her own, and we supported her 100%. However, I think champagne was involved in our somewhat impulsive decision to have two weddings!

The SS Rotterdam, "The Grande Dame" of the Holland American Cruise Line

Mom wore her special blue dress to meet all the captains.

Always have a martini before dinner!

Dancing before dinner

Charlene and Mom

Mom and Dino

Nora and George

"Take Five" with Dave Brubeck on the jazz cruises

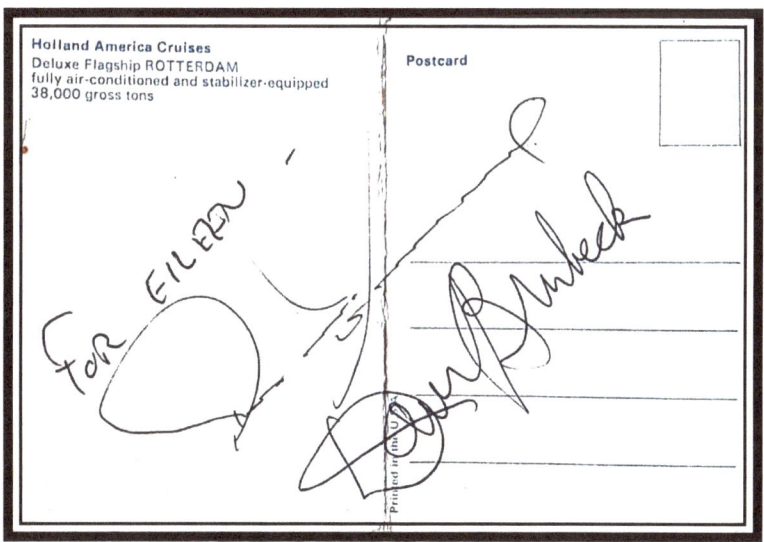

For Eileen – Dave Brubeck

Charlene, Mom, and Nora – perennial mariners

Chapter 9

"THE MOST BEAUTIFUL WOMAN I EVER SAW"

On the way to the ceremony, with eyes welled up with tears, my mother's husband-to-be uttered, "She's the most beautiful woman I ever saw!" We had just picked up a gorgeous corsage for my mother and were on our way to gather together for the special event.

Mom had already lived a very full life – more than most. During the years "after The Doctor," she was on her own, financially and otherwise. However, she loved life and was always ready for the next adventure. She went to work for the City of Springfield in the schools and in the fire department. She mastered doing the payroll for 300 firefighters, and their schedules were different each week. She did it by hand with no computer! Quite a feat! She worked her way up to become Administrative Assistant to the Chief. While working there, she formed a great friendship with one of her co-workers, Betty, and her two sisters, Peggy and Joyce. Soon she was an honorary member of their very large Italian family.

Mom was quite busy all the time. Her goal was always to be a perennial student, so she continually signed up for classes in cooking, cake decorating, the Italian language, symbolism in literature, etc. She joined groups like The Grange and became their Chaplain! As a member of the Red Hat Society, she met monthly and wore red hats and purple to echo the sentiment in the poem by Jenny Johnson.

Warning

When I am an old woman I shall wear purple
With a red hat which doesn't go and doesn't suit me.
But maybe I ought to practice a little now?
So people who know me are not too shocked and surprised
When suddenly I am old and start to wear purple.

"When I am an old woman I shall wear purple"
Mom and Dino

THE MOST BEAUTIFUL WOMAN I EVER SAW

Over the years, my mother met a couple of suitors with whom she might have considered marriage. One was a retired teacher and military sergeant who took her sailing every weekend. He was an excellent ballroom dancer, and they danced the nights away at a former military base in the area. Another was an eye doctor who also excelled at ballroom dancing and convinced her to wear contact lenses. (It took her ten years to convince me!) Both relationships went on for a few years but nothing serious ever developed.

Living alone didn't suit her. She loved being with people especially since the three of us were inseparable for most of our lives. So, at one point, Mom went to live with my sister, Nora, in the small country town where The Doctor had lived for most of his life. She lived with her in a beautiful, historic home for ten years, and my sister told her they were the best years of my sister's life. My mother had her own quarters, but the house didn't have many modern conveniences. My sister often worried about turning up the furnace or using electric devices that might cause a fire. She was also very cautious about strangers coming into the home (like Cable people) who might try to steal some of their antiques and unique pieces of art. We often joked that my mother got married so that she could have heat and Cable TV!

Mom met Bob on one of the senior bus trips. They sat together, and she learned that his wife had just died. They became great companions and drove to all the neighboring towns each week to play cards. Bob wanted to marry Mom. He said if she would cook for him, he would do all the cleaning. Mom introduced him to us, and we thought the whole idea was great. Bob was such a kind, gentle man. He had a great personality, a wonderful sense of humor, and he loved animals and trains. He loved to eat lunch at a nearby restaurant called the Steaming Tender where you could see trains go by all afternoon. I think of Bob every time I see a train! He also loved the weather and created daily charts and albums with newspaper articles and pictures reporting on unique weather events like the "Great New England Hurricane of 1938, one of the deadliest storms in recorded history." I still have his scrapbooks. You couldn't ask for a nicer person. He even had relatives who came over on the Mayflower! And, he had a house with lots of heat and all the super-premium channels available on cable!

We planned an intimate wedding with just the six of us – Mom, Bob, Nora, me, and our two husbands, George and Dino. In a neighboring town, there was a beautiful historic inn that was just perfect for the event – The Horatio Lyon House. It was a Greek Rivival style home built in the early 1800s. We rented out a small part of the inn so that we could have the ceremony in the living room, a special dinner in the dining room, and a beautiful cake and after-dinner cordials in another area. We hired a justice of the peace, and "Love Is a Many Splendored Thing" played in the background as Nora and I walked Mom down the aisle. It was a wonderful evening – so wonderful that we decided we should do it all over again and have a party this time! We may have had a little champagne to help us with our decision.

Exactly one month later, we did it. This time we rented the entire inn. We designed beautiful invitations and sent them to close family members and friends – 36 in all. Several sterling silver candelabras (which we brought to the affair) and linens graced all the tables. Numerous courses of delicious food were carefully chosen. The wine was flowing and so was the after-dinner cognac. We called the same justice of the peace and asked if we could do it all over again. He chuckled and said it wasn't against any laws. We stood in front of a large winding staircase and greeted our guests in the foyer as they arrived. We said, "no gifts" unless they would like to bring a bottle of wine for the couple's new wine cellar. Extravagant selections of wine, port, and champagne filled the room reserved for the cake. We drank them for years! It was beautiful. We couldn't believe we almost missed this opportunity for such a great party. No one knew this was a "replay" of the first event. It could have caused a little confusion on anniversaries. We just decided to celebrate both dates.

Mom and Bob had about twenty great years together. They loved cruising and went to the Mediterranean, Panama, the Holy Land, and more. When they weren't traveling, all of us ate leisurely dinners together most evenings which always lasted two or more hours.

Nora and George's house with Mom's purple irises

Mom and George

Private wedding for the family

THE MOST BEAUTIFUL WOMAN I EVER SAW 189

Mom and Bob exchange rings

The reception

Mom, Bob, and their guests at the wedding

Bob and Mom cruising the Mediterranean

Shopping at the souk in Morocco

Nora bought a dress from the souk in Casablanca.

Mom continued to wheel and deal. When a developer decided to build some homes down the road, she figured out that he could buy some of their land and create a "U" which would allow them to build more homes. The developer loved the idea!

She also had an eBay business in her eighties! There was a big factory in town which made designer lingerie for all of the big companies like Vanity Fair and Victoria's Secret. The public was allowed to purchase items wholesale. Mom bought tons of lace-trimmed satin sets of lingerie and sold them on eBay to people around the world. My sister taught her how to set up lights to photograph the items, and she learned how to add the right amount of postage from the computer. Mail carriers picked up everything at her door. She had an exciting little business to supplement The Fund!

Mom still had a real zeal for life. Some health problems slowed her down a little bit, but she continued to have way more energy than us. We couldn't keep up with her. On one of the cruises to the Middle East, she tripped going off the bus and fell down right on her knees. She got a knee replacement in one, but some "cardiac episodes" during surgery prevented her from having the other knee replaced. As a result, she was in pain a lot but never gave up. No more ballroom dancing.

After twenty years, Bob developed Alzheimer's Disease. At times, he didn't remember my mother. During the night, he was often startled because he thought she was a stranger who had broken into the house. At other times, he thought Mom was his mother which worked out really well because he loved his mother so much. He used to tell Mom that she was the best mother anyone could have. Eventually, he had to join a memory unit in an assisted living facility. It was getting a little scary when he thought Mom was an intruder.

At one point, we took him back home because he really wanted to leave with us every time we visited. It was heartbreaking. He didn't understand why he couldn't come with us. We thought we would try it out for a week. However, he was more distraught at home. He kept trying to drive his car to see his mother who had died several decades earlier. We had to bring him back to the memory unit, but we visited him on a daily basis. The nurses were astounded that he had so much company.

Mom was on her own in an isolated house in the country. My sister and I alternated and spent every evening with her until 8:00 or 9:00. We always ate dinner together, but we didn't like the idea of her being alone during the night. People came in to help her with household responsibilities, but she was still on her own during the day when we worked. She started taking senior transportation to various clubs where she could play cards and socialize. However, the bus rides were very long because they would pick up people in several towns before arriving at the final destination. We wanted her to move to a retirement community. The trouble was finding the right one.

We tried them all out – even moved her lock, stock, and barrel into one of them. It was a gorgeous apartment, and we bought all new furniture. Then she decided she wanted to go back home. We agreed that it didn't live up to our expectations, so we tried again. We ate dinner at most of them, but the dining rooms were so quiet you could hear a pin drop. It was terrible.

Finally, we found the perfect place. It was an independent living retirement community called Keystone. We all went to dinner in a very large dining room about fifty by one hundred feet. Everyone was so friendly. "Hi! Are you moving in? Sit over here near us." They ALL introduced themselves. It was so festive.

She had a gorgeous apartment with a full kitchen, laundry, large living room, two bedrooms, and two full baths. She used the second bedroom for an office. There was a central lobby where everyone congregated when they picked up their mail or headed down to various functions. We discovered that we could purchase meal tickets, so we all ate dinner together every night. It was just like dining on a cruise ship with all the different courses, and we could bring our own wine! A group of French people sat next to us regularly, and we called them *The French Connection*. They often arranged luncheons where they served French food and taught us the language. We also met Danny, an old family friend of George's uncle, and we invited him to dine with us every evening. He was a great guy, and he had so many entertaining stories to tell us. We all got to know everyone in the whole place.

On Saturdays, we'd go down to the dining room for brunch. We could order any kind of omelet, the best bacon I've ever tasted, other breakfast specialties, Danish pastry, and orange

juice which we supplemented with Vodka to make screwdrivers. After brunch, we'd head to the lobby for a live concert with some very talented musicians. Then we'd go to the movies in the theater. They had everything. It was great.

During the evenings, Mom played cards with various groups of people or went to art classes. She actually became a very talented artist. We have ten beautiful paintings that she did. Many more activities and trips were held on a daily basis along with lots of live entertainment and special parties. It was the best thing that ever happened to us. We all felt like we wanted to move in. My mother kept going, going, going. It was still hard to keep up with her. The only sad part of Keystone was when ambulances arrived. Word spread like wildfire. It was scary for all the residents since they knew that most who left in an ambulance never came back. One day, it happened to Mom.

During the last week of my mother's life, Nora and George happened to celebrate Nora's birthday with Mom three days early. It was a Tuesday. On Wednesday, I took her to an appointment, and we went out to eat at **Napoli** where we heard "**Al Di La**," our favorite Italian song. The next morning, Mom died. She was up early getting coffee. Her heart must have given out. It was three months before her **ninety-sixth** birthday! Although her husband, Bob, didn't understand what had happened, he died one month later. It's as if he sensed she was gone.

A few days earlier, my husband, Dino, told her that he would take care of her cat if anything happened to her. It was the one unsettled matter in her life. As soon as she knew Mr. Milo would have a home, she died right after that. Mom made provisions for everything else – her funeral, her obituary, and the cemetery plots. We often took a ride to the cemetery, and she would show us the plots – one for all six of us. We always knew where she would be buried. At least we thought we did. With Mom - always the unexpected!

Mom became an artist in her nineties!

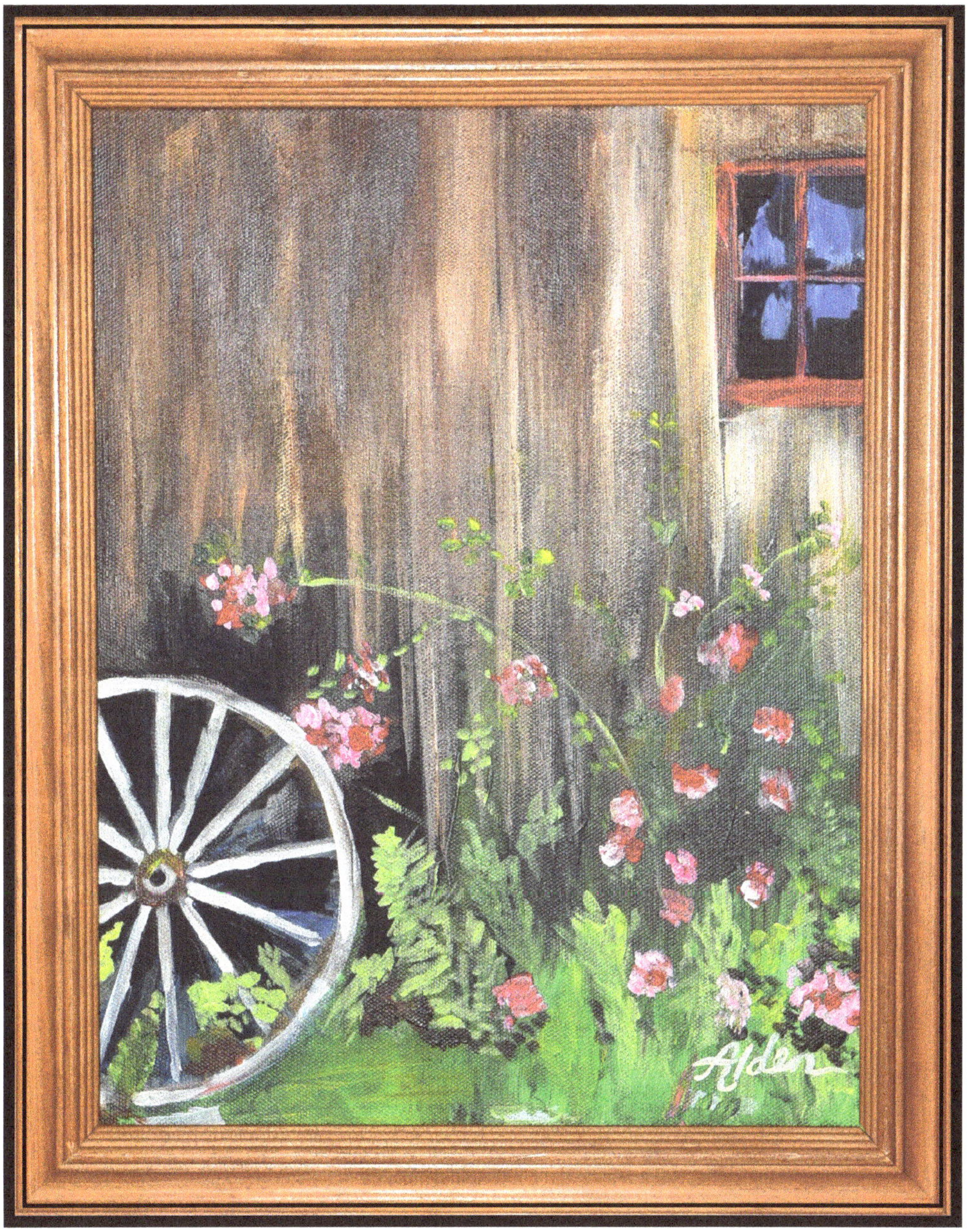
Alden

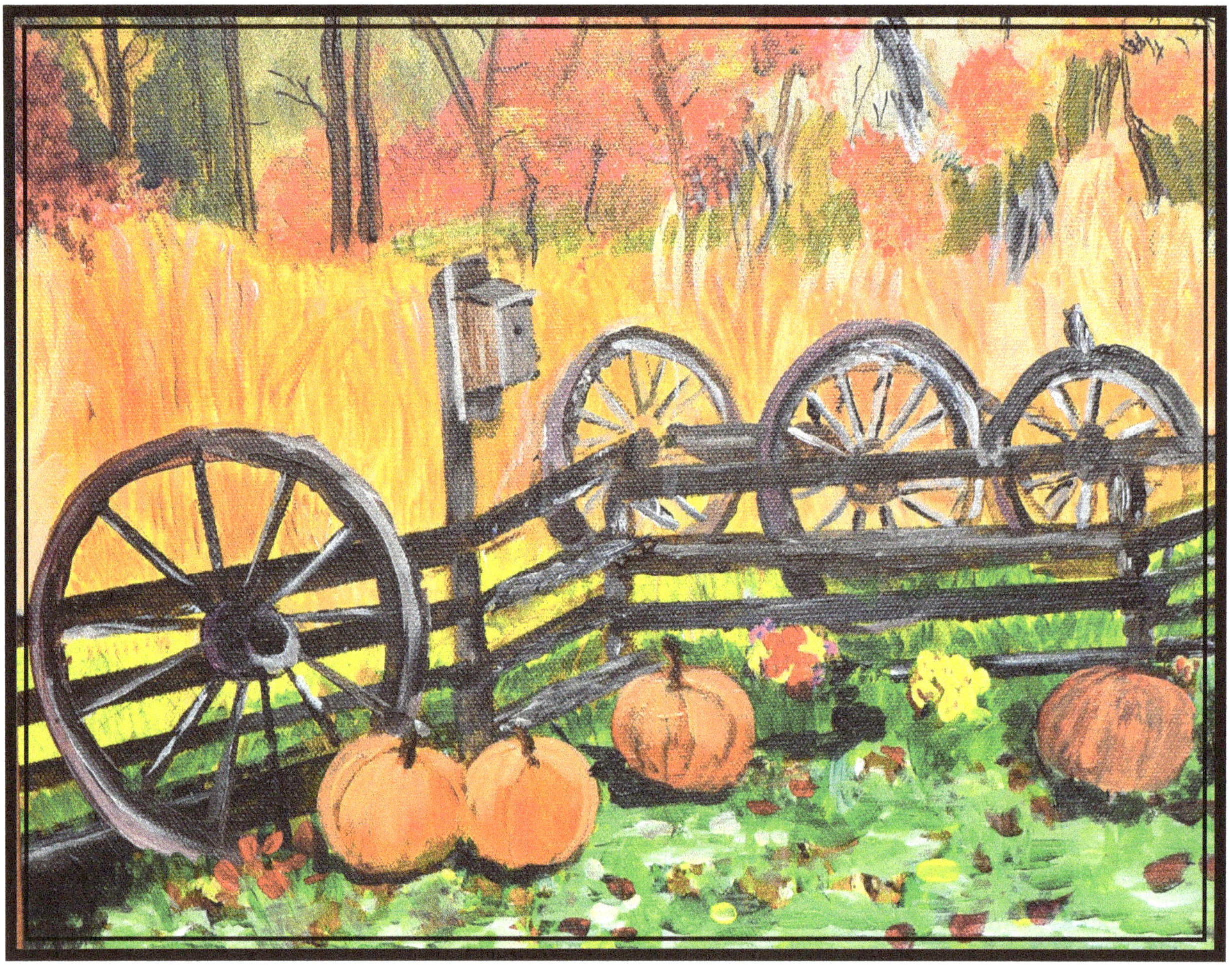

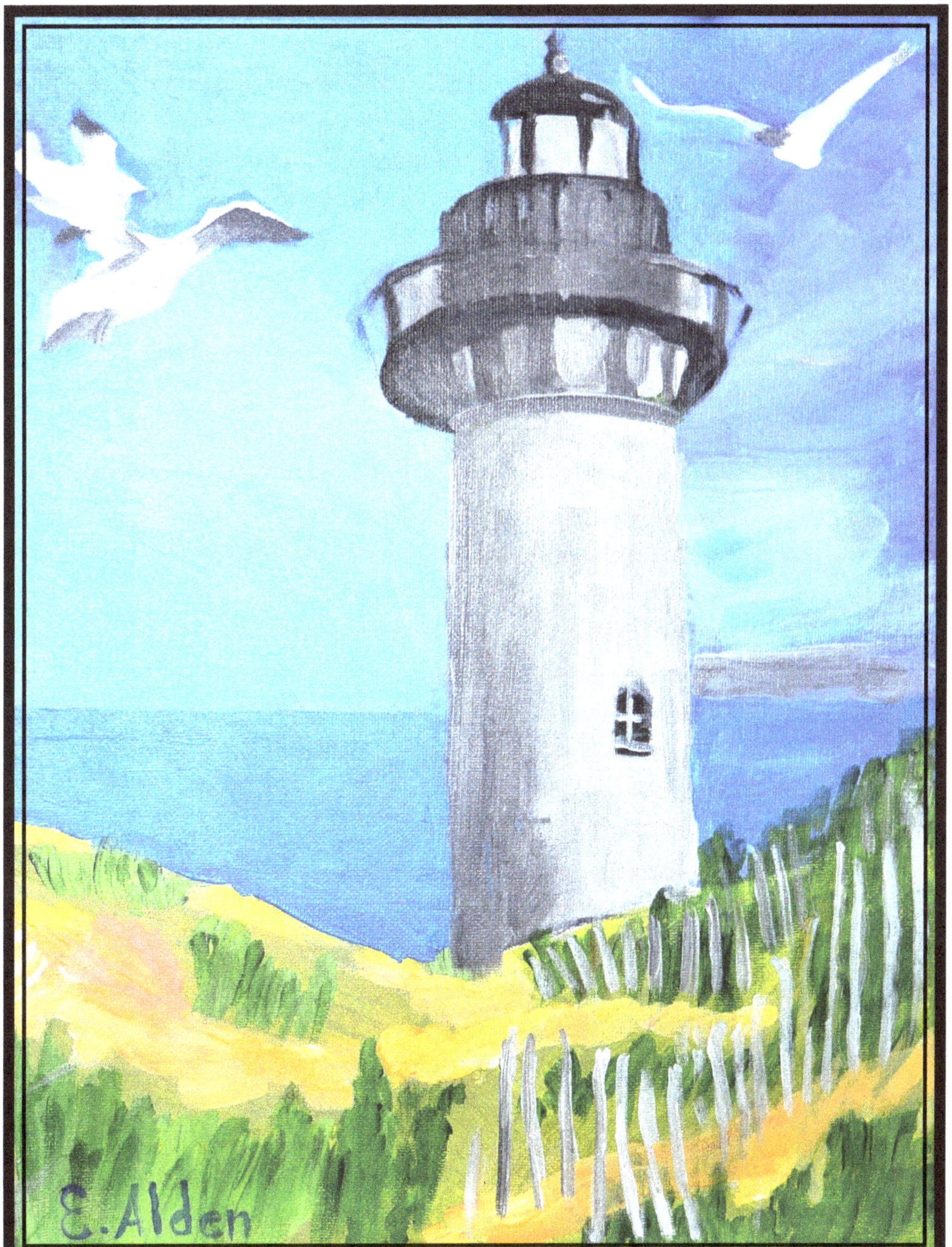
E. Alden

Mr. Milo liked to hide under the covers.

Mr. Milo

Robert E. Alden (1923 – 2017)

Robert E. Alden (1923 – 2017) Bob grew up in Springfield and Belchertown, raised by his mother, Sarah, and her sister, Olive. After walking home from Technical High School during the hurricane of 1938 Bob became interested in the weather, and kept accurate records of weather conditions for the next 60 years. He served in the US army and then worked as a foreman at the Springfield Post Office for 33 years. He retired to Ludlow and built a home on the location of his family's sawmill property, and even had the street named after him. He and his wife, Eileen Alden, traveled and cruised extensively, all over the U.S. and Europe, many times bringing Eileen's 2 daughters, Nora and Charlene, with them. Bob always loved cats, and in all of the photos of Bob growing up, there was a cat next to him. He traveled to see lighthouses and covered bridges, and loved trains. Close to 4 PM each afternoon he would go to see the trains come through Three Rivers, MA.

Chapter 10

"MOST OF ALL, WE REMEMBER MOM"

Planning the funeral took some time. We wanted it to be just right. We often thought of having a "final" party before she died. We wanted her friends to see her alive, but we couldn't quite decide what to do. Then, it was too late. Mom was gone, and we needed to arrange a funeral.

Mom never wanted an open casket. She said it would be better to remember our loved ones as we knew them. We agreed. Everything else she requested was in place – the funeral home, the cost, the cemetery plot, and apricot-colored roses in a spray across the casket – everything except the gravestone. When she was alive, we thought about choosing one every time we passed a business that sold monuments. Somehow, it seemed too real, too final. We didn't want to get that close to death.

Mom didn't care for funeral parlors, so we decided to have the memorial talk right at the cemetery. It was a beautiful old cemetery out in the country town where The Doctor and all of us had lived at one time or another. We took a ride to see our six family plots once again before the big day and asked them to cut the grass so that everything would be presentable.

We decided this very special event would be private, so we sent out invitations to close friends and family members. When you're ninety-six years old, not too many friends are left.

My mother outlived them all! The Hampden House restaurant, **La Cucina**, was just down the road from the Old Cemetery. It seemed like the perfect place for the reception. We sampled everything and chose a menu for 36 guests. We told the hostess we would like six tables for six with red and white wine on each table that should be continually replenished throughout the afternoon.

Mom had written her own obituary, and we included it on the invitation. She asked my husband, Dino, to prepare the funeral discourse. Several religions were represented among the guests, and my mother's primary concern was that all would be comfortable and encouraged. After relating some of the outstanding experiences and accomplishments in Mom's life, he focused on the resurrection – *anástasis* – a hope they all had in common.

We asked the funeral parlor to make arrangements with the cemetery for 36 chairs to be placed under a tent at the gravesite. Mom had other special requests, and we put them all in place. We brought a collage with all the memorable photos to the restaurant ahead of time. There were pictures of Mom in her wedding dress with her first husband, a man whose name we carried but who was also a mystery to us. She married him just before he shipped out for World War II. There were pictures of Mom and The Doctor and more with Bob, the husband with whom she spent her golden years. Pictures of Sylvie and Charles were included, and of course, her two girls were there along with our husbands, Dino and George. Everything was set, or so we thought!

Finally, the big day arrived, and we all drove separately to the Old Cemetery. It was a beautiful fall day with blue skies and a temperature that was pleasantly warm. We drove up to the little cul-de-sac next to the gravesite that we had visited many times. **Nothing was there! No people. No tent. Nothing!**

We glanced to the side and saw small groups of people congregating under a tent up on a small hill about fifty yards away. We were paralyzed for a moment. Somehow, we seemed to glide up the incline toward a gravesite we had never seen before. I saw my sister, and we just stared at each other wide-eyed. We didn't know what to say or do! **They were burying my**

mother in the wrong place! It was like a force kept pulling us toward the site, and we fell into place in the front row. We were in a daze. We greeted friends while a thousand thoughts were streaming through our minds. What should we do? Should we say something? Would she have to be exhumed when everything was corrected? We just sat down and went with the flow. We can't wait to tell her what happened when we see her again. Even in her death, Mom was taking us on another adventure.

The funeral discourse was beautiful. It's so much more meaningful when someone who really knew the deceased recounts the special moments in the person's life. It was touching, funny, sad, even inspiring to reminisce and to hear about the fascinating woman who was our mother.

After the talk, a friend sang "Danny Boy." It was my mother's request. It was heart-rending and beautiful. One version of the music contained alternative lyrics to be sung to a woman, "Eily Dear," but we weren't able to work it out. It would have been perfect because my mother's name was Eileen.

> Oh, Danny Boy, the pipes, the pipes are calling
> From glen to glen, and down the mountainside,
> The summer's gone, and all the roses falling,
> It's you, it's you must go and I must bide.
> But come ye back when summer's in the meadow,
> Or when the valley's hushed and white with snow
> Tis I'll be here in sunshine or in shadow,
> Oh, Danny Boy, Oh Danny Boy, I love you so!

Then, as they slowly lowered the casket into the ground, a Bagpiper sauntered up over the hill and disappeared into the distance playing "Auld Lang Syne" – a mournful song about old friends remembering the adventures they had together. When I think about that moment, it still brings tears to my eyes.

> Should auld acquaintance be forgot
> And never brought to mind?
> Should auld acquaintance be forgot
> And the days of auld lang syne?
> For auld lang syne, my dear
> For auld lang syne
> We'll drink a cup of kindness yet
> For the sake of auld lang syne

It was perfect – all we could have hoped for. Mom would have been happy. Then, in her honor and style, we all departed for a long, leisurely lunch where we remembered Mom.

In time, we purchased a stone for her grave. It actually took a few years because we had to reach an agreement with the cemetery regarding the six plots. Although Nora had land deeds with precise plot descriptions, they insisted that two were in one place and four were in another part of the cemetery. None were in the area my mother picked out years earlier that we visited so many times. Well, we didn't want to move her, and we liked her final resting place. We came to an agreement, but then the pandemic closed everything down for two years. Finally, we selected a simple, but beautiful, stone and engraved some words from one of her favorite poems that defined how she lived her long, full life.

> If thou of fortune be bereft,
> and in thy store there be but left
> two loaves, sell one, and with the dole,
> buy hyacinths to feed thy soul.
> John Greenleaf Whittier

What we remember most about Mom was her love for life. She lived for almost a century, but she just wanted to keep going day and night. She always said she was "on borrowed time." I think our love kept her alive. It was impossible to keep up with her even though she was in pain a great deal of the time near the end. Her body was giving out, but her mind was as sharp as ever. (I attribute that to all the reading she did throughout her life.) Mom's idea of slowing down was to do just one or two things on our outings instead of several. Of course, she insisted that we always include our favorite pastime - a leisurely lunch or dinner.

Did I mention that she was a beautiful woman? Mom just didn't age! She had ivory skin (she hid from the sun most of her life). Her blue eyes glistened and turned steel gray when she was excited - outdone only by her lovely Irish smile. When Mom was younger, she had striking, auburn hair. In her later years, it was pure white! Stunning! Yes, she was lovely, but it was her warmth and compassion that made her so attractive.

On a personal note, we cherished the emotional support Mom provided whenever we encountered various challenges in life. Sometimes she would offer a solution, but most of the time she just listened for hours. I think she knew that it helped us to order our thoughts.

Our mother was fearless, adventurous, optimistic, resilient, and generous. She was passionate about knowledge. When we were young, every week she posted a new vocabulary word on a small blackboard in the kitchen, and then she used the word all week. "Facetious" was one. No matter what we said, she would respond, "Surely, you're being facetious (light-hearted, humorous, droll)." Mom also loved animals – always had one or two throughout her life (sometimes more).

What made her unique? Mom was far ahead of her time – by light-years! I don't know if we appreciated it when we were young. She just seemed normal to us. I guess we thought all mothers were like her. But, as we got older, we realized that Mom was a bit more eccentric than most. She was a free thinker and must have been extremely intelligent – genius level! Who else could memorize and recite so many epic poems with hundreds of lines? She even created her own version of shorthand and made meticulous notes about everything in life which she filed in triplicate and in a special book she called "Matters of Consequence" (from *The Little Prince*). She always told us to "Write things down! You won't remember. You think you will, but you won't." She was right. In the business world, she went up against the best of them defying tradition and breaching circles that were forbidden to the fairer sex. She was probably the most courageous person we knew. She was undaunted! How aptly Mom epitomized the sentiments of Elizabeth Cady Stanton, the 19th century leader in the women's rights movement:

Mom and her two girls

"I have wandered in the latitudes beyond the prescribed sphere of women."

Mom's legacy to us was The Fund – the concept of having a contingency plan, not just financial, but in all areas of life. That's not to say she didn't appreciate the benefits of having cash on hand. Small stashes of money were always hidden in secret compartments in her pocketbook and in small bank accounts around the city. Even when we were very young, she gave us a $50 bill to hide in our clothing for emergencies. We never left the house without it. We still do that today. So, we understood the need for a cash reserve. However, The Fund provided much more than financial security. It inspired us to grasp every opportunity, to embrace each adventure, and to share those experiences with others as our mother did all of her life.

Like most, Mom may have had some shortcomings, but to us, she was absolutely perfect! That's what we remember most about Mom.

The Old Cemetery in Hampden, Massachusetts

ACKNOWLEDGEMENTS

This memoir would not have been possible without the recollections and guidance of my sister, Nora Kane. She worked with me throughout the process, reading drafts, making suggestions, and filling in the gaps.

I am also thankful to friends and family members who were willing to read first drafts and to provide feedback for the early chapters – Sylvie Nagel Pressman, Elizabeth (Eli) Rivera, Gladys Evertsz, and Ann Chaffee. Sylvie, being a prime member of the "cast" also brought back to mind memories and fine details that I had forgotten. My sister's husband, George Eliopoulos, provided keen insight about human nature and about my mother's character.

Finally, I want to thank my staunch supporter – my husband, Dino Diaz. He read and reread, critiqued and commended, and motivated me to persevere and to publish. Dino also provided most of the photos and edited our childhood pictures from the early days. I will always be indebted to him for helping me to create The Fund.

APPENDICES

MOM'S ORATORY REPERTOIRE – ALL RECITED FROM MEMORY

GUNGA DIN by Rudyard Kipling

You may talk o' gin and beer
When you're quartered safe out 'ere,
An' you're sent to penny-fights an' Aldershot it;
But when it comes to slaughter
You will do your work on water, An' you'll lick the bloomin' boots of 'im that's got it.

Now in Injia's sunny clime,
Where I used to spend my time A-servin' of 'Er Majesty the Queen,
Of all them blackfaced crew

The finest man I knew Was our regimental bhisti, Gunga Din,

He was 'Din! Din! Din!
'You limpin' lump o' brick-dust, Gunga Din!
'Hi! Slippy *hitherao*
'Water, get it! *Panee lao,*
'You squidgy-nosed old idol, Gunga Din.'
The uniform 'e wore
Was nothin' much before,
An' rather less than 'arf o' that be'ind,
For a piece o' twisty rag An' a goatskin waterbag Was all the field equipment 'e could find.
When the sweatin' troop-train lay

In a sidin' through the day,
Where the 'eat would make your bloomin' eyebrows crawl,
We shouted 'Harry By!'
Till our throats were bricky-dry,
Then we wopped 'im 'cause 'e couldn't serve us all.

It was 'Din! Din! Din!
'You eathen, where the mischief 'ave you been?
'You put some *juldee* in it
'Or I'll *marrow* you this minute
'If you don't fill up my helmet, Gunga Din!'
'E would dot an' carry one
Till the longest day was done; An' 'e didn't seem to know the use o' fear.
If we charged or broke or cut, You could bet your bloomin' nut,
'E'd be wait in' fifty paces right flank rear.
With 'is mussick on 'is back,
'E would skip with our attack,
An' watch us till the bugles made 'Retire,'
An' for all 'is dirty 'ide
'E was white, clear white, inside
When 'e went to tend the wounded under fire! It was 'Din! Din! Din!'
With the bullets kickin' dust-spots on the green. When the cartridges ran out,
You could hear the front-ranks shout, 'Hi! ammunition-mules an' Gunga Din!'
I shan't forgit the night
When I dropped be'ind the fight With a bullet where my belt-plate should 'a' been. I was chokin' mad with thirst,
An' the man that spied me first
Was our good old grinnin', gruntin' Gunga Din.
'E lifted up my 'ead,
An' he plugged me where I
bled,

An' 'e guv me 'arf-a-pint o' water green.
It was crawlin' and it stunk,
But of all the drinks I've drunk,
I'm gratefullest to one from Gunga Din.

It was 'Din! Din! Din!
''Ere's a beggar with a bullet through 'is spleen; ''E's chawin' up the ground, 'An' 'e's kickin' all around:
'For Gawd's sake git the water, Gunga Din!'

'E carried me away
To where a dooli lay,
An' a bullet come an' drilled the beggar clean.
'E put me safe inside,
An' just before 'e died, 'I 'ope
you liked your drink,' sez Gunga Din.

So I'll meet 'im later on
At the place where 'e is gone—
Where it's always double drill and no canteen.
'E'll be squattin' on the coals
Givin' drink to poor damned souls, An' I'll get a swig in hell from Gunga Din!

Yes, Din! Din! Din!
You Lazarushian-leather Gunga Din!
Though I've belted you and flayed you, By the livin' Gawd that made you,

You're a better man than I am, Gunga Din!

SPARTACUS TO THE GLADIATORS

BY ELIJAH KELLOGG

SPARTACUS: **Ye call me chief; and ye do well to call him chief who for twelve long years has met upon the arena every shape of man or beast the broad Empire of Rome could furnish, and who never yet lowered his arm.** If there be one among you who can say that ever, in public fight or private brawl, my actions did belie my tongue, let him stand forth and say it. If there be three in all your company dare face me on the bloody sands, let them come on. And yet I was not always thus,— a hired butcher, a savage chief of still more savage men. My ancestors came from old Sparta and settled among the vine-clad rocks and citron groves of Syrasella. My early life ran quiet as the brooks by which I sported; and when, at noon, I gathered the sheep beneath the shade, and played upon the shepherd's flute, there was a friend, the son of a neighbor, to join me in the pastime. We led our flocks to the same pasture and partook together our rustic meal. One evening, after the sheep were folded, and we were all seated beneath the myrtle which shaded our cottage, my grandsire, an old man, was telling of Marathon and Leuctra; and how, in ancient times, a little band of Spartans, in a defile of the mountains, had withstood a whole army. I did not then know what war was; but my cheeks burned, I know not why, and I clasped the knees of that venerable man, until my mother, parting the hair from off my forehead, kissed my throbbing temples, and bade me go to rest, and think no more of those old tales and savage wars. That very night the Romans landed on our coast. I saw the breast that had nourished me trampled by the hoof of the war-horse, the bleeding body of my father flung amidst the blazing rafters of our dwelling! To-day I killed a man in the arena; and, when I broke his helmet-clasps, behold! he was my friend. He knew me, smiled faintly, gasped, and died;—the same sweet smile upon his lips that I had marked, when, in adventurous boyhood, we scaled the lofty cliff to pluck the first ripe grapes, and bear them home in childish triumph! I told the prætor that the dead man had been my friend, generous and brave; and I begged that I might bear away the body, to burn it on a funeral pile, and mourn over its ashes. Ay! upon my knees, amid the dust and blood of the arena, I begged that poor boon, while all the assembled maids and matrons, and the holy virgins they call Vestals, and the rabble, shouted in derision, deeming it rare sport, forsooth, to see Rome's fiercest gladiator turn pale and tremble at the sight of that piece of bleeding clay! And the prætor drew back as I were pollution, and sternly said, "Let the carrion rot; there are no noble men but Romans." And so, fellow gladiators, must you, and so must I, die like dogs. O Rome! Rome! thou hast been a tender nurse to me. Ay! thou hast given to that poor, gentle, timid shepherd lad, who never knew a harsher tone than a flute-note, muscles of iron and a heart of flint; taught him to drive the sword through plaited mail and links of rugged brass, and warm it in the marrow of his foe;—to gaze into the glaring eyeballs of the fierce Numidian lion, even as a boy upon a laughing girl! And he shall pay thee back, until the yellow Tiber is red as frothing wine, and in its deepest ooze thy life blood lies curdled! Ye stand here now like giants, as ye are! The strength of brass is in your toughened sinews, but tomorrow some Roman Adonis, breathing sweet perfume from his curly locks, shall with his lily fingers pat your red brawn, and bet his sesterces upon your blood. Hark! hear ye yon lion roaring in his den? 'Tis three days since he has tasted flesh; but to-morrow he shall break his fast upon yours, and a dainty meal for him ye will be! If ye are beasts, then stand here like fat oxen, waiting for the butcher's knife! If ye are men, follow me! Strike down yon guard, gain the mountain passes, and there do bloody work, as did your sires at old Thermopylæ! Is Sparta dead? Is the old Grecian spirit frozen in your veins, that you do crouch and cower like a belabored hound beneath his master's lash? **O comrades! warriors! Thracians! If we must fight, let us fight for ourselves! If we must slaughter, let us slaughter our oppressors! If we must die, let it be under the clear sky, by the bright waters, in noble, honorable battle!**

MEMORIAL TALK FOR EILEEN KANE ALDEN

(PRESENTED BY DINO DIAZ)

On behalf of the family, Nora, Charlene, George, Sylvie, Charles, and myself, I would like to welcome you and thank you for being here today to support and encourage us. Eileen loved life, and she wanted us to celebrate her life and the wonderful times we spent together.

Eileen was a very special person in the lives of many, especially in the lives of those who are here today. I've known Eileen for the past thirty-six years, but many here have known her a lot longer than that. After all, she lived almost an entire century! She would have been ninety-six years old in November. She had a lot of wonderful friends, rich experiences, and valuable wisdom that she passed on to all of us. I'm sure you would agree that she was a fascinating woman.

For example, did you know that she was a fantastic ballroom dancer? I saw her dance - beautiful, graceful, light on her feet. She looked like Ginger Rogers without exaggeration. She wrote poetry and could also recite lengthy, epic poems from memory often bringing people to tears. In her later years, she became an excellent artist. She could also hear a melody one time and then immediately play an elaborate version of the song on the piano. Nora and Charlene used to say that their mother played piano by ear, but rarely played life by the rules because she was so spontaneous and adventurous. And, that's what they loved most about her.

Here's another example. One time she saw an advertisement in the New York Times for an apartment in Rome on the Via Veneto, the most famous street that you often see in Hollywood films about Italy. She thought it would be a great adventure for her and her girls. But, she mixed up the zeros in the money conversion and realized it wasn't $100 a month - like she thought - but closer to $10,000 a month! - a very hefty price even today, but especially back in the late

APPENDICES 225

sixties. Another time, she considered buying a castle in Orvieto, a mountaintop village one hour north of Rome. Eileen, Nora, and Charlene actually went there for a few weeks to assess the property, and they returned with some incredible stories that we talked about often over the years.

Eileen didn't buy the castle, but she did become the owner of Rahar's Inn, a famous hotel in Northampton, closely associated with Smith College and President Calvin Coolidge. During this real estate phase, she also sold the "Big House" in Hampden, the home of Dr. Charles Furcolo. When no one else could sell it, she said, "I will!" and she actually sold it twice! She put a huge ad in the New York Times and received a call from a man named Edwin Donald Snider.

As the story goes, he wanted to tour the property and asked if she would meet him at Bradley Field since he didn't know anyone in the area. When he arrived, a huge group of people crowded around him looking for autographs. She wondered what was going on since he had never been here before. His business partner said, "You don't follow baseball, do you? That's Duke Snider, 'The Silver Fox.' He just won the World Series with the Brooklyn Dodgers!"

Around the same time period, she was involved with the purchase of a race track called Berkshire Downs. Apparently there were some problems, and she landed on the front page of the Springfield Newspaper being sued with Frank Sinatra and Dean Martin! (I have the article) So, you can imagine, life was never dull for Nora and Charlene because Eileen took them everywhere she went.

She loved plants and grew beautiful gardens wherever she lived. She also loved animals and often brought all the strays home. In fact, one of her greatest concerns was what would happen to her cat, "Mr. Milo." Ironically, just a few days before she died, I told her that if anything ever happened to her, I would take him. She was so happy, because Eileen was the type of person who tried to have all arrangements in place in life so that she would never be a burden to her loved ones.

Eileen especially loved people, and she often brought them home to stay, as well. One time she met a French college girl named Sylvie Nagel who was here from France to teach a special summer French course. When Eileen met Sylvie and found out she was going to stay at the YWCA for the entire summer, she brought her home to live with them instead. Sylvie became part of the family and that was the beginning of a lifelong relationship.

Eileen also loved music, especially jazz. She took her daughters on many jazz cruises (Later, she took the whole family.) She met Dave Brubeck, Sarah Vaughn, Dizzy Gillespie and other jazz stars several times. She loved all types of music - Ray Charles, Patsy Cline - she even had a signed autograph from James Brown - who signed it, "To Eileen, a real soul sister."

Somewhere in the middle of all of these experiences, she was a Registered Nurse and worked for Dr. Furcolo for 30 years - first in surgery in the operating room with him and then in the Furcolo Clinic. She also worked at the Springfield School Department and the Springfield Fire Department where she retired as the Administrative Assistant to the Chief. She made wonderful, lifelong friends at both places and only retired to get married at the age of 75! She married a great man, Bob Alden, who was very kind and who loved her very much. They were able to have many great years together. Her daughters were so happy because she had been a widow for most of her life, working very hard to raise her two daughters alone. That must have been difficult at times but going through life together - just the three of them - created a very special bond that remained throughout their lives.

You can imagine how much they will miss her. ALL of us will miss her beautiful smile, her love for life, and those long, leisurely dinners with good wine and great stories just like some of the ones you heard today.

So, it's natural for us to wonder, will we ever be able to see Eileen again - to resume the enjoyable times that we had together? The faithful man, Job, asked the same question. In the Bible Book bearing his name, at Job 14:14, he asked, "If a man dies, can he live again?" What was the answer? The next verse tells us:

Job 14:15 "You will call, and I will answer you. You will LONG for the work of your hands."

In other words, Job said that his Creator would long, or yearn, to see the work of his hands, his creations, people like Eileen. He has preserved every aspect of her being in his memory - her look, her walk, her smile, her thoughts, her memories of us. That's why those who have passed away are spoken of as being in the "memorial tombs." Yes. Eileen is in God's memory.

What will happen next? The Bible tells us in the Gospel of John, Chapter 5 and Verses 28, 29.

"Do not be amazed at this, for the hour is coming in which ALL those in the memorial tombs will hear his voice and come out."

How will that happen? The Bible tells us that our Creator, Jehovah God, has given his only begotten Son, Jesus Christ, the authority, the power, and the incredible privilege of resurrecting those who have died. That's why Jesus described himself this way at John 11:25:

"I am the resurrection and the life. The one who exercises faith in me, even though he dies, will come to life."

When Jesus said those words, he was speaking to Martha, the sister of his great friend, Lazarus, who had just died. Jesus traveled to see the family because he was about to resurrect their brother and bring him back to life. Interestingly, during the account, Jesus used a very appropriate illustration to describe death. Notice what he said, as the account continues.

"Lazarus our friend has fallen ASLEEP, but I am traveling there to awaken him.' Jesus, however, had spoken about his DEATH. But they imagined he was speaking about taking rest in sleep. Then Jesus said to them plainly: 'Lazarus has died."

Here, Jesus compared death to sleep for a number of reasons. When a person is in a deep sleep, he is at peace. He is not thinking, not suffering, but most importantly, when someone is asleep, he will WAKE UP! And, that is the exact definition of the Greek word for resurrection:

A NA STA SIS - a raising up or a standing up

Yes, that is the comforting promise that we have here today. Eileen will "stand up." We will be able to greet her, hug her and resume the wonderful life we had with her. Can you imagine what that will be like? When Jesus resurrected a little girl in the Gospel of Mark, chapter 5 and Verse 42, notice how the people reacted:

"And at once they were beside themselves with great ecstasy."

GREAT ECSTASY! That is exactly how we are going to feel when we welcome back Eileen and we all begin to live what the Bible calls, "the real life," life under perfect conditions for eternity! Yes, at that time, death, the "last enemy," will be brought to nothing - just as the Book of Revelation promises in Chapter 21 and Verse 4:

"And he will wipe out every tear from their eyes, and death will be no more, neither will mourning nor outcry nor pain be anymore. The former things have passed away."

We hope that reflecting on the hope & promises from the Scriptures has been comforting to all here today because the Bible assures us that we will have the opportunity to see Eileen again. I'd like to say a prayer at this time.

It was Eileen's request that we hear one of her favorite songs, Danny Boy. Bruce Sprecht will do that for us, and then the Bagpiper will conclude the service.

NOTES

Preface

- I Remember Mama By *Michael Rich* — Comment — Updated August 11, 2023 https://fiftiesweb.com/tv/i-remember-mama/

Introduction

- "The best protection any women can have…is courage." https://www.azquotes.com/author/14012-Elizabeth_Cady_Stanton
- The Hardship of Accounting By Robert Frost https://archive.org/details/poetryofrobertfr0000fros_l8o7

Chapter One - Mexico

- Why Does a Southern Drawl Sound Uneducated to Some? By R. Douglas Fields; December 7, 2012 https://blogs.scientificamerican.com/guest-blog/why-does-a-southern-drawl-sound-uneducated-to-some/
- Hey, Y'all: Southern Accents Voted Most Attractive By Jessica Roy November 11, 2013 https://newsfeed.time.com/2013/11/11/hey-yall-southern-accents-voted-most-attractive/
- The Court of the Two Sisters https://www.courtoftwosisters.com/about-us/our-history
- "Court of Two Sisters" restaurant, Royal Street, French Quarter; May, 2007 Photo by Infrogmation https://creativecommons.org/licenses/by/2.5/
- Xochimilco Floating Gardens of Mexico City By Suzanne Barbezat, May 3, 2019; Facchecked by Erin Medlicott; tps://www.tripsavvy.com guide-to-xochimilco-1589073
- Some Like It Hot; Wikipedia® June 24, 2024 Creative Commons Attribution-ShareAlike License 4.0; https://en.wikipedia.org/wiki/Some_Like_It_Hot

Chapter Two – Rome

- A Brief History of the Croque Monsieur, France's Cheese Toastie; culture trip By **Alex Ledsom;** February 8, 2017 https://theculturetrip.com/europe/france/articles/a-brief-history-of-the-croque-monsieur-frances-cheese-toastie
- Croque Monsieur: BY: Nagi; April 30,2021; Updated on October 4, 2021 https://www.recipetineats.com/croque-monsieur-french-ham-cheese-sandwich/
- *Charade*: Wikipedia® January 7, 2024 Creative Commons Attribution-ShareAlike License 4.0; https://en.wikipedia.org/wiki/Charade_(1963_film)
- Mona Lisa: Wikipedia® January 15, 2024 Creative Commons Attribution-ShareAlike License 4.0; https://en.wikipedia.org/wiki/Mona_Lisa
- L'Air du Temps (perfume): Wikipedia® January 16, 2023
- Creative Commons Attribution-ShareAlike License 4.0; https://en.wikipedia.org/wiki/L%27Air_du_Temps_(perfume)
- L'Air du Temps Dusting Powder; tps://www.ebay.com/itm/125337251990?var=0&mkevt=1&mkcid=1&mkrid=711-53200-19255-h0&campid=5338590836&toolid=10044&customid=71ffdf2463c0102ec29bba82ef2356851/2024
- Marcel Proust: Wikipedia® Creative Commons Attribution-ShareAlike License 4.0 01/15/2024 https://en.wikipedia.org/wiki/In_Search_of_Lost_Time#Memory
- Moses (Michelangelo) Wikipedia® 10/19/2023; Creative Commons Attribution-ShareAlike License 4.0; https://en.wikipedia.org/wiki/Moses_(Michelangelo)
- Romulus and Remus; Wikipedia® January 4, 2024 Creative Commons Attribution-ShareAlike License 4.0
- Roman guardians: the untold story of Rome's 200+ Colosseum cats (2023)TRAVELING CATS By Vanessa; April 29, 2015 https://traveling-cats.com/2015/04/colosseum-cats-rome.html
- *The Way of the Dragon;* Wikipedia® January 9, 2024; Creative Commons Attribution-ShareAlike License 4.0; https://en.wikipedia.org/wiki/The_Way_of_the_Dragon
- Spanish Steps Wikipedia® February 25, 2024; Creative Commons Attribution-ShareAlike License 4.0; https://en.wikipedia.org/wiki/Spanish_Steps

- Sorelle Fontana; April 1, 2023; Wikipedia® Creative Commons Attribution-ShareAlike License 4.0; https://en.wikipedia.org/wiki/Sorelle_Fontana
- Victor Emmanuel II Monument; Wikipedia® January 11, 2024; Creative Commons Attribution-ShareAlike License 4.0; https://en.wikipedia.org/wiki/Victor_Emmanuel_II_Monument
- Trevi Fountain; December 11, 2023; Wikipedia® Creative Commons Attribution-ShareAlike License 4.0; https://en.wikipedia.org/wiki/Trevi_Fountain
- *La Dolce Vita;* Wikipedia® January 7, 2024; Creative Commons Attribution-ShareAlike License 4.0; https://en.wikipedia.org/wiki/La_Dolce_Vita
- The Lion Sleeps Tonight; Wikipedia® June 16, 2024; Creative Commons Attribution-ShareAlike License 4.0; https://en.wikipedia.org/wiki/The_Lion_Sleeps_Tonight

Chapter Three – 3 B's and a Con Man; The Beach, The Berkshires, Boston

- *Burgers, Dogs and History;* By Christopher Brooks; July 1, 2011; New York Times https://www.nytimes.com/2011/07/03/nyregion/harrys-place-a-historic-drive-in-review.html
- Breck Shampoo Wikipedia; September 30, 2023; Creative Commons Attribution-ShareAlike License 4.0; https://en.wikipedia.org/wiki/Breck_Shampoo
- There Was a Little Girl; Wikisource February 26, 2024; Creative Commons Attribution-ShareAlike License 4.0; https://en.wikisourcc.org/wiki/There_Was_a_Little_Girl
- The Sopranos; ; Wikipedia® June 27, 2024; Creative Commons Attribution-ShareAlike License 4.0; https://en.wikipedia.org/wiki/The_Sopranos
- Berkshire Downs; Wikipedia® May 27, 2020; Creative Commons Attribution-ShareAlike License 4.0;https://en.wikipedia.org/wiki/Berkshire_Downs_(racetrack)
- *Rhapsody in Blue;* Wikipedia® December 11, 2023; Creative Commons Attribution-ShareAlike License 4.0; https://en.wikipedia.org/wiki/Rhapsody_in_Blue
- Isabella Stewart Gardner Museum theft; Wikipedia® ; March 16, 2024; Creative Commons Attribution-ShareAlike License 4.0; https://en.wikipedia.org/wiki/Isabella_Stewart_Gardner_Museum

- Union Oyster House; Wikipedia® June 24, 2024; Creative Commons Attribution-ShareAlike License 4.0; https://en.wikipedia.org/wiki/Union_Oyster_House
- Durgin-Park; Wikipedia® January 24, 2024; Creative Commons Attribution-ShareAlike License 4.0; https://en.wikipedia.org/wiki/Durgin-Park
- Jacob Wirth; Wikipedia® June 26, 2024; Creative Commons Attribution-ShareAlike License 4.0; https://en.wikipedia.org/wiki/Jacob_Wirth_Restaurant
- Locke-Ober; Wikipedia® April 28, 2024; Creative Commons Attribution-ShareAlike License 4.0; https://en.wikipedia.org/wiki/Locke-Ober
- The Marliave; Wikipedia® October 4, 2020; Creative Commons Attribution-ShareAlike License 4.0; https://commons.wikimedia.org/wiki/File:Marliave_Restaurant_-_Boston,_MA_-_DSC04737.JPG
- Parker House; Wikipedia® April 3, 2023; Creative Commons Attribution-ShareAlike License 4.0; https://en.wikipedia.org/wiki/Parker_House

Chapter Four – Rahar's Inn

- Rahar's Inn; http://www.historic northampton.org/members_only/histimages/FormB/hnformb786.pdf
- The Northampton Book; p. 369; The City of Northampton, Massachusetts; 1954
- https://ia601000.us.archive.org/24/items/northamptonbookc00unse/northamptonbookc00unse.pdf
- *What'd I Say;* Wikipedia® October 27, 2022; Creative Commons Attribution-ShareAlike License 4.0; What'd I Say (album) - Wikipedia
- *Wooly Bully;* Wikipedia® December 26, 2023; Creative Commons Attribution-ShareAlike License 4.0; Wooly Bully - Wikipedia
- *Hard Hearted Hannah* (The Vamp of Savannah); Wikipedia® December 29, 2023; Creative Commons Attribution-ShareAlike License 4.0; Hard Hearted Hannah (The Vamp of Savannah) - Wikipedia
- Dale Carnegie; Wikipedia® July April 11, 2024; Creative Commons Attribution-ShareAlike License 4.0; https://en.wikipedia.org/wiki/Dale_Carnegie

Chapter Five – Sylvie

- *You Can't Take It with You* (play) Wikipedia® December 27, 2023; Creative Commons Attribution-ShareAlike License 4.0; https://en.wikipedia.org/wiki/You_Can%27t_Take_It_with_You_(play)
- *My Family and Other Animals* Wikipedia® July 12, 2023; Creative Commons Attribution-ShareAlike License 4.0; https://en.wikipedia.org/wiki/My_Family_and_Other_Animals
- *The Little Prince* Wikipedia® January 22, 2004; Creative Commons Attribution-ShareAlike License 4.0; https://en.wikipedia.org/wiki/The_Little_Prince
- *Palace of Castel Gandolfo* Wikipedia® June 6, 2022; Creative Commons Attribution-ShareAlike License 4.0; https://en.wikipedia.org/wiki/Palace_of_Castel_Gandolfo

Chapter Six – Albert

- Robert H. Goddard; Wikipedia; January 17, 2024; Creative Commons Attribution-Share Alike License 4.0; https://en.wikipedia.org/wiki/Robert_H._Goddard
- Duke Snider - Wikipedia; January 15, 2024; Creative Commons Attribution-Share Alike License 4.0; https://en.wikipedia.org/wiki/Duke_Snider
- Mont Blanc; Wikipedia; December 1, 2023; Creative Commons Attribution-Share Alike License 4.0; https://en.wikipedia.org/ wiki/Mont_Blanc
- *All I Really Need to Know I Learned in Kindergarten;* Wikipedia; January 8, 2024; Creative Commons Attribution-Share Alike License 4.0; https://en.wikipedia.org/wiki/All_I_Really_Need_to_Know_I_Learned_in_Kindergarten

Chapter Seven – Bats in the Belfry; The Clinic

- Lost New England; Monarch Life Insurance Company Building, Springfield, Mass by Derek Strahan; July 20, 2020 https://lostnewengland.com/2020/07/monarch-life-insurance-company-building-springfield-mass/

- *1812 Overture* Wikipedia® January 24, 2024; Creative Commons Attribution-Share Alike License 4.0; https://en.wikipedia.org/ wiki/1812_Overture
- Venice; Wikipedia® January 28, 2024; Creative Commons Attribution-Share Alike License 4.0 https://en.wikipedia.org/wiki/Venice
- Dark Eyes (Russian song) Wikipedia; December 12, 2023; Creative Commons Attribution-Share Alike License 4.0; https://en.wikipedia.org/wiki/Dark_Eyes_(Russian_song)
- Castello del Poggio – Guardea; Umbria Tourism; https://www.umbriatourism.it/en/-/castello-del-poggio-guardea-en
- Lucrezia Borgia Wikipedia®; December 12, 2023; Creative Commons Attribution-Share Alike License 4.0; https://en.wikipedia.org/ wiki/Lucrezia_Borgia
- Orvieto – What an Italian Hill Town Should Be; Rick Steves' Europe; https://www.ricksteves.com/watch-read-listen/read/articles/orvieto-what-an-italian-hill-town-should-be
- *Orvieto* Wikipedia® December 11, 2023; Creative Commons Attribution-Share Alike License 4.0; https://en.wikipedia.org/ wiki/Orvieto
- Big Yellow Taxi; Wikipedia®; December 19, 2023; Creative Commons Attribution-ShareAlike License 4.0; https://en.wikipedia.org/wiki/Big_Yellow_Taxi

Chapter Eight – How People Grieve

- John Greenleaf Whittier Wikipedia®; January 3, 2024; Creative Commons Attribution-Share Alike License 4.0; https://en.wikipedia.org/wiki/John_Greenleaf_Whittier
- Chapter Nine – The Most Beautiful Woman I Ever Saw
- Jenny Johnson Wikipedia®; December 26, 2023; Creative Commons Attribution-Share Alike License 4.0; https://en.wikipedia.org/ wiki/Jenny_Joseph
- 1938 New England Hurricane Wikipedia®; February 9, 2024; Creative Commons Attribution-Share Alike License 4.0; https://en.wikipedia.org/wiki/1938_New_England_hurricane

Chapter Ten – Most of All, We Remember Mom

- Danny Boy Wikipedia; January 26, 2024; Creative Commons Attribution-Share Alike License 4.0; https://en.wikipedia.org/ wiki/Danny_Boy
- Auld Lang Syne Wikipedia; January 25, 2024; Creative Commons Attribution-Share Alike License 4.0; https://en.wikipedia.org/ wiki/Auld_Lang_Syne
- John Greenleaf Whittier Wikipedia; January 3, 2024; Creative Commons Attribution-Share Alike License 4.0 https://en.wikipedia.org/wiki/John_Greenleaf_Whittier
- Elizabeth Cady Stanton Wikipedia; January 19, 2024; Creative Commons Attribution-Share Alike License 4.0; https://en.wikipedia.org/ wiki/Elizabeth_Cady_Stanton
- Eighty Years and More; Reminiscences 1815-1897 by Elizabeth Cady Stanton; Project Gutenberg; December 26, 2020; Public domain in the USA https://www.gutenberg.org/ebooks/11982

PHOTO CREDITS

Chapter One

- Sami99tr, New Orleans French Quarter, New Orleans, Louisiana, March 18, 2009, CC BY-SA 3.0 DEED, via https://commons.wikimedia.org/wiki/File:French_Quarter03_New_Orleans.JPG
- Nuggehalli2015, Alamo Mission in San Antonio, April 15, 2016,
- Creative Commons Attribution-Share Alike 4.0 International,via https://commons.wikimedia.org/wiki/File:The_Alamo_2016.jpg
- Mark Bonica from Durham, NH, USA, The San Antonio River Walk, July 21, 2010,
- https://creativecommons.org/licenses/by/2.0/,viahttps://commons.wikimedia.org/wiki/File:The_San_Antonio_River_Walk_%284816836941%29.jpg
- Bruno Cortés FP, Facade of the National Autonomous University of Mexico, CC0 1.0 Public DomainCC0 https://www.pexels.com/photo/facade-of-the-national-autonomous-university-of-mexico-16485916/
- Floating Gardens Xochimilco, CC0 1.0 Public Domain, https://pxhere.com/es/photo/1039529

Chapter Two

- Nikada, Eiffel Tower in Paris, France, Eiffel Tower in Spring, February 26, 2018, https://www.gettyimages.com/detail/photo/eiffel-tower-in-paris-france-royalty-free-image/924894324?adppopup=true
- Grand Hôtel & Café de la Paix, September 14, 2008, Canonical URL https://creativecommons.org/licenses/by-sa/2.0/, via Parishttps://commons.wikimedia.org/wiki/File:Grand_H%C3%B4tel_%26_Caf%C3%A9_de_la_Paix_1.jpg

- Jebulon, a "bouquiniste" by the Seine, in Paris, France, May 29, 2010, Canonical URL https://creativecommons.org/licenses/by-sa/3.0/, via https://commons.wikipedia.org/wiki/File:Bouquinistes_seine2.jpg
- P. Vasiliadis, Michaelangelo Moses, June 9, 2006, Canonical URL https://creativecommons.org/licenses/by-sa/3.0/, via https://commons.wikimedia.org/wiki/File:Michaelangelo_Moses.jpg
- The Best of Rome Nightlife, harry's bar roma for @bduperrin, August 28, 2009, Canonical URL https://creativecommons.org/licenses/by-nd/2.0, via URL: www.tripify.com/blog/the-best-of-rome-nightlife debs-eye, Colosseum, cat sleeping, February 19, 2008, Canonical URL https://creativecommons.org/licenses/by/2.0/, via https://www.flickr.com/photos/debbcollins/2310630426
- Dino Diaz, The Spanish Steps in Rome at the top of Via Condotti – the Rodeo Drive of Rome
- Nico De Pasquale Photography, Ariel View of Piazza Venezia and Altare della Patria, Rome, October 22, 2020, https://www.gettyimages.com/detail/photo/aerial-view-of-piazza-venezia-and-altare-della-royalty-free-image/1281637891?adppopup=true
- Nick Brundle Photography, The Trevi Fountain at Piazza Di Trevi, Rome, Italy. August 29, 2020, gettyimages.com/detail/photo/trevi-fountain-rome-italy-royalty-free-image/1270054112?phrase=fountain+of+trevi+nick+brundle+photography&adppopup=true
- London, CC0 Public Domain, https://pxhere.com/en/photo/661722

Chapter Three

- Dino Diaz, Harry's Place in Colchester, Connecticut
- The crowd watches a race at Berkshire Downs, September, 1960, The Berkshire Eagle Days Gone By: Images of Berkshire Downs from the Eagles Archives, https://www.berkshireeagle.com/history/berkshire-downs-days-gone-by/collection_acae3786-a170-11ec-87c3-bfcfa1df1647.html,
- Purchased from: https://mng-neni.smugmug.com/Berkshire-Eagle-Archive-Photos/Days-Gone-By-Scenes-from-Berkshire-Downs/i-CZbLhHx

- Berkshire Downs, October 11, 1960, the final day of the 1960 race season, The Berkshire Eagle Days Gone By: Images of Berkshire Downs from the Eagles Archives, https://www.berkshireeagle.com/history/berkshire-downs-days-gone-by/collection_acae3786-a170-11ec-87c3-bfcfa1df1647.html,
- Purchased from: https://mng-neni.smugmug.com/Berkshire-Eagle-Archive-Photos/Days-Gone-By-Scenes-from-Berkshire-Downs/i-CZbLhHx
- Arthur Bowes, Ye Olde Union Oyster House, Boston, MA, October 11, 2020, Canonical URL https://creativecommons.org/licenses/by-sa/4.0/, via https://commons.wikimedia.org/wiki/File:Ye_Olde_Oyster_House.jpg
- Beyond My Ken, Swan Boats tied up in the Lagoon of the Boston Public Garden, March 13, 2019, Canonical URL https://creativecommons.org/licenses/by-sa/4.0/, via https://commons.wikemedia.org/wiki/File:2017_Boston_Public_Garden_Swan_Boats_from_southwest.jpg
- Sean Dungan, Courtyard, Isabella Stewart Gardner Museum, November 11, 2017, Canonical URL https://creativecommons.org/licenses/by-sa/4.0/, via https://commons.wikimedia.org/wiki/File:Courtyard,_Isabella_Stewart_Gardner_Museum,_Boston.jpg
- The Fairmont Copley Plaza Hotel, Dino Diaz
- TanRo, The Boston Public Library McKim Building shines at night in Copley Square, March 23, 2016, Creative Commons Attribution-Share Alike 4.0 International license, via https://commons.wikimedia.org/wiki/File:Boston_Public_Library%27s_McKim_Building_at_Night.jpg
- Dino Diaz, The Boston Public Library

Chapter Four

- Dino Diaz, Rahar's Inn today
- Dino Diaz, Our grandmother's house
- Dino Diaz, Our townhouse in the Mattoon Street Historic District

Chapter Six

- Dino Diaz, The Doctor's house in the center of town
- Dino Diaz, We called it The Big House; others called it The Castle
- Bowman Gum, Brooklyn Dodgers centerfielder Duke Snider, https://commons.wikimedia.org/wiki/File:Duke_Snider_1953.jpg, via http://www.vintagecardtraders.org/virtual/53bowman_color/53bowman_color.html
- Lu Brito, Road from Grenoble to Chamonix-Mont Blanc, May 3, 2016, Creative Commons *Attribution-Share Alike 4.0 International*, via https://commons.wikimedia.org/wiki/File:Estrada_de_Grenoble_para_Chamonix-Mont_Blanc.jpg
- Patryk Hejduk, Cobbled Old Tremola Road to the St Gotthard, August 10, 2020, passhttps://commons.wikimedia.org/wiki/File:Old_Tremola_Road.jpg, Creative Commons *Attribution-Share Alike 4.0 International*, via https://commons.wikimedia.org/wiki/File:Old_Tremola_Road.jpg
- Ghazarians, Mohammad Reza Pahlavi, 1973, Public Domain, https://commons.wikimedia.org/wiki/File:Mohammad_Reza_Pahlavi.png

Chapter Seven

- Mohan Nannapaneni, Photo of a White American Eskimo Dog on Green Grass, CC0 Public Domain, via https://www.pexels.com/photo/photo-of-a-white-american-eskimo-dog-on-green-grass-7237824/
- Adriano, *Arcobaleno ad Orvieto* (A Rainbow in Orvieto), July 13, 2006, https://creativecommons.org/licenses/by-sa/3.0/ via https://commons.wikimedia.org/wiki/File:Arcobaleno_ad_Orvieto.JPG
- Chait Goli, Orvieto, Umbria, Italy, Brown Concrete Building, CC0 Public domain, via https://www.pexels.com/photo/brown-concrete-building-2031966/
- Zyance, Orvieto: handicraft, September, 2006, Creative Commons Attribution-Share Alike 2.5 Generic license via https://commons.wikimedia.org/wiki/File:Orvieto_souvenir_z02.jpg

- Dino Diaz, We carried home dinner service for eight
- Edosangio, Castello del Poggio di Guardea, March 4, 2017, Creative Commons *Attribution-Share Alike 4.0 International*, via https://commons.wikimedia.org/wiki/File:Castello_del_Poggio_di_Guardea.jpg
- Dino Diaz, Venice, The floating city
- Dino Diaz , Enchantment in Venice

Chapter Eight

- Dino Diaz, Family gravesite in New Haven, Connecticut
- kees torn, July 4, 2015, https://creativecommons.org/licenses/by-sa/2.0/https:/ via commons.wikimedia.org/wiki/File:Rotterdam_%28ship,_1997%29_001.jpg
- Dino Diaz, Mom sailed 500,000 miles on the Holland America Cruise Line
- Dino Diaz, Mom wore her special, blue dress to meet all the Captains

Chapter Nine

- Dino Diaz, Mom became an artist in her nineties

Chapter Ten

- Dino Diaz, The Old Cemetery in Hampden, Massachusetts

Eileen Kane Alden